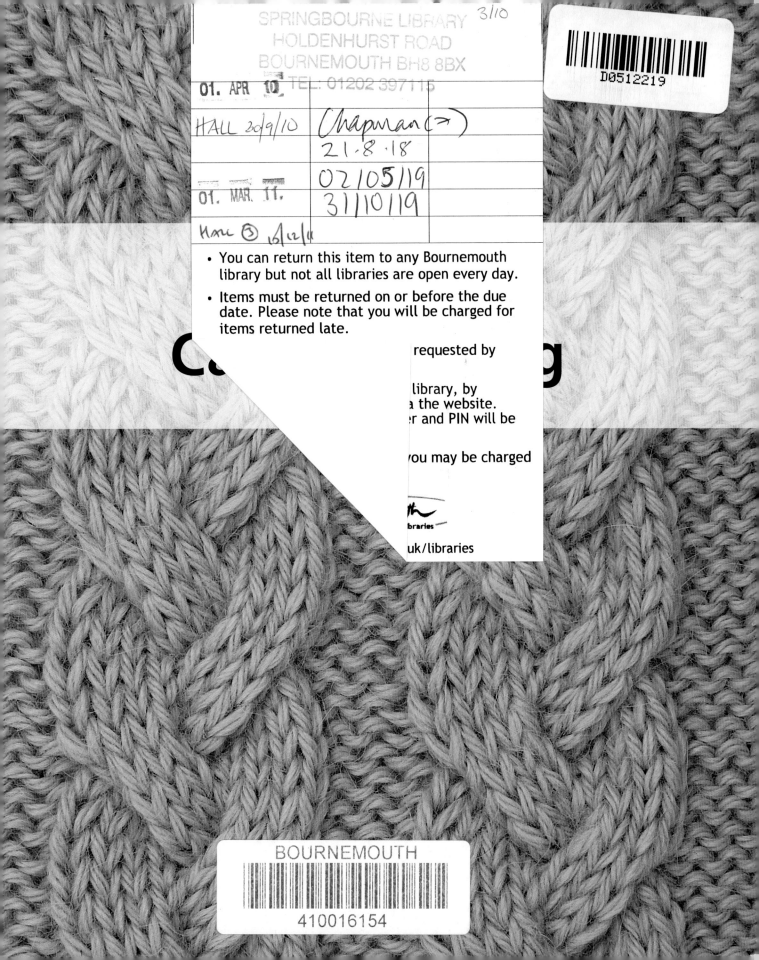

C   g

requested by

library, by
a the website.
er and PIN will be

ou may be charged

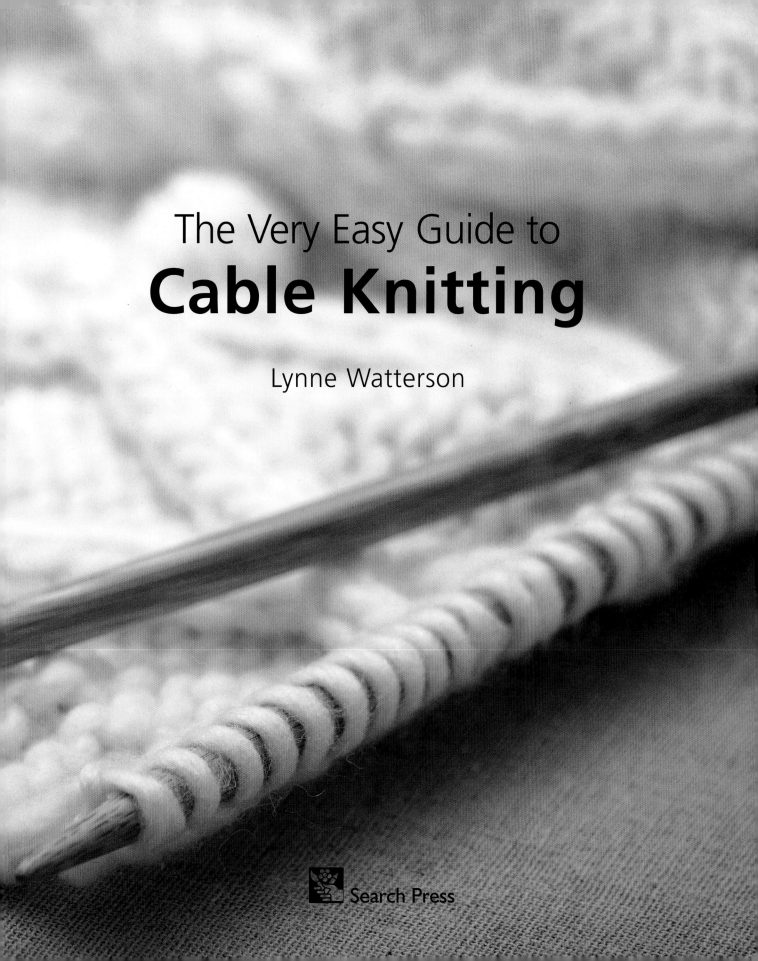

The Very Easy Guide to
Cable Knitting

Lynne Watterson

Search Press

A QUARTO BOOK

Published in 2010 by Search Press Ltd
Wellwood
North Farm Rd
Tunbridge Wells
Kent TN2 3DR

ISBN: 978-1-84448-531-4

Conceived, designed and produced by
Quarto Publishing plc
The Old Brewery
6 Blundell Street
London
N7 9BH

QUAR.ECW

Senior editor: Katie Hallam
Copy editor: Liz Dalby
Art director: Caroline Guest
Art editor: Jackie Palmer
Designer: Tania Field
Photographer: Lizzie Orme
Illustrator: Kate Simunek

Creative director: Moira Clinch
Publisher: Paul Carslake

Colour separation by PICA Digital Pte
Ltd, Singapore
Printed in Singapore by Star Standard
Pte Ltd

10 9 8 7 6 5 4 3 2 1

contents

introduction

This book has been written for knitters with a passion for sumptuous texture, sculptured cables and tactile yarns. It will encourage beginners through to intermediate and experienced knitters to pick up their needles and get knitting.

The simple-to-follow lessons take you through the process of knitting, from the wide variety of beautiful yarns available and the basic tools required to knit them, the knitting basics – cast on, cast off, knit and purl – to perfect seaming and finishing touches that add that all-important finish.

The cables are divided into three lessons: Mock cables, Cable panels and Cable patterns. Each lesson opens with an essential cable technique in a simple step-by-step format – featuring written instructions and clear photographs.

The techniques are followed by a selection of stunning stitch patterns worked in a range of natural yarns – including pure wool, wool tweed, natural undyed wool, alpaca and mohair. The stitch patterns can be used to practise cable techniques, design your own projects or to substitute the stitch patterns used for the projects in this book – remember to check the tension carefully if you are substituting a pattern.

To complete each lesson, a collection of simple stylish projects has been designed using a selection of the stitch patterns. The designs are worked in an appealing palette of cream, stone, soft grey, charcoal and mocha, with accents of duck egg, lavender and soft green.

I dedicate this book to my wonderful mum. I have cherished memories of the hours we spent together knitting and sewing. Thank you for your relentless love and support. I miss you.

about this book

This book guides you through the entire process of cable knitting, from the very basics of knitting, through the different stitches and patterns, to making projects with the perfect finish.

lessons

Twenty-one lessons teach you all you need to know, with step-by-step artworks and photography to ensure clarity.

Written patterns provide clear instruction

Charts provide a quick visual reference

Perfectly knitted examples show the individual stitches and the overall pattern

Pattern rows are highlighted with markers for additional clarity

Step-by-step photography breaks down the instructions into easy-to-follow parts, showing close-ups of essential detail

the cables

Large swatches of the different stitches feature throughout, with all the information you need to emulate the design.

Good-sized examples show clearly individual stitches and the overall pattern

Needle size and yarn information is given throughout

Easy-to-follow patterns and charts provide the essential instructions

projects

Put everything you've learnt into practice and make beautiful items for you and your home.

Patterns, materials lists and size and tension details provide the essential information you need to make your chosen item

Concise instructions guide you through the finishing process/ additional elements

Photographs show the end product and suggest uses/ placements

Understanding the patterns and charts

For a key to the abbreviations used in the patterns and the symbols used in the charts, turn to page 140.

Yarn information

The details of the specific yarn used in each project are supplied on page 144, but you can choose your own yarns, following the yarn type given next to the symbol on the sample pages.

Finishing

To find out how to add a professional and decorative finish to your projects, and how to care for them once they're in use, turn to pages 126–139.

lesson 1 | yarns

Knitting yarns are usually produced by spinning fibres together. There are two main categories of fibre – natural and synthetic. Natural fibres are divided into two categories: animal and vegetable. Animal fibres include wool, angora, cashmere and silk; vegetable fibres include cotton, linen and ramie.

The stitch samples and projects in this book have been made using natural fibres to show the stitch patterns off to their best advantage and to enhance the texture and durability of the projects.

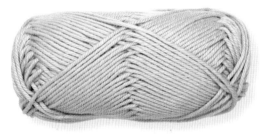

Wool is the yarn most commonly associated with knitting. Spun from the fleece of sheep, it has many excellent qualities – durability, elasticity and warmth. It is available in a wide range of colours, as well as 100 per cent undyed virgin wool.

Cotton is a soft, natural plant fibre that grows around the seeds of the cotton plant. The yarn produced by spinning the fibres is ideal for all seasons – warm in the winter and cool in the summer. Cotton gives a special crispness to patterns, making the detail stand out well, but it tends to lack resilience. The wide colour range available includes naturals, soft shades and bright, zingy colours. Mercerized cotton is chemically treated to make it more lustrous and less liable to shrink.

Cashmere is the wool or fur of the Kashmir goat. The finest cashmere comes from the underbelly and the throat of the goats, with a lesser grade coming from the legs and back. The belly and throat areas produce longer fibres, making the wool particularly soft, while the shorter fibres from the legs and back are heavier. The natural colours are white, grey and brown, but the wool is easily dyed and is available in a wide range of colours.

understanding yarn labels

The band or label attached to yarn gives you important information about the yarn, helping you to make the right choice for your project. In a prominent position on the band you will find the company logo followed by the yarn name and its knitted weight. The band also tells you what the yarn is made from, the length and weight of yarn in the ball, the shade and dye lot numbers, the recommended knitting needle sizes and, in some cases, the recommended knitted tension (see page 22). Aftercare and washing instructions are shown by a list of symbols (see page 139).

It is important to use yarn from the same dye lot for a project, as slight differences in colour could be noticeable in the finished piece.

Care instructions

Recommended needle size(s) for stocking stitch

Recommended knitted tension

90% Merino wool 10% Cashmere — Fibre content

Length and weight — 42m / 50g

Yarn name — Debbie Bliss **como**

Shade and dye lot numbers — Colour: **19003** Dyelot: 3 8

ROWAN
handknit cotton
100% COTTON 100% BAUMWOLLE 100% COTON

Rowan Yarns
Holmfirth
England
H548000
50g

In accordance with
B.S. 984
Approx Length 85m
(93 yds)
www.knitrowan.com

Machine wash
Warm iron
Do not bleach
Dry cleanable in all solvents
Do not tumble dry
Dry flat out of direct sunlight

CARE INSTRUCTIONS
Dry clean or hand wash in soapflakes; do not soak; cool rinse; do not wring; short spin; do not leave wet; reshape and dry flat away from direct sunlight; use damp pressing cloth.

Chemisch reinigen oder handwäsche mit geeignetem Waschmittel; nicht einweichen; kühl und gründlich ausspülen; nicht auswringen; kurz anschleudern; nicht nass liegenlassen; in form ziehen und flach liegend trocknen vor direkter Sonnen und hitzeeinwirkung schützen; mit feuchtem Tuch dämpfen.

Nettoyage à sec ou lavage à main avec des paillettes de savon; ne pas laisser tremper; rinçage froid; ne pas tordre; essorage court; ne pas laisser mouillé; redonner la forme et laisser sécher à plat à l'abri du soleil; repasser à vapeur.

Synthetic fibres such as acrylic, polyester and polyamide are derived from coal and petroleum products and are spun in various ways to resemble natural fibre yarns. These yarns are usually machine washable; however, care should be taken when blocking and pressing – too much heat will cause the knitting to lose its shape and the stitch pattern its crispness.

Tip

Keep one label as a reference with the tension swatch in a safe place, together with any leftover yarn and spare buttons. The label can be referred to when washing the item and spare yarn and buttons can be used for repairs.

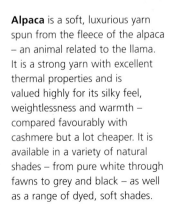

Alpaca is a soft, luxurious yarn spun from the fleece of the alpaca – an animal related to the llama. It is a strong yarn with excellent thermal properties and is valued highly for its silky feel, weightlessness and warmth – compared favourably with cashmere but a lot cheaper. It is available in a variety of natural shades – from pure white through fawns to grey and black – as well as a range of dyed, soft shades.

yarn weights

Yarns are available in many different weights or thicknesses – from very fine to extra-bulky. Your chosen pattern will tell you which weight of yarn is required and the needle sizes used to achieve the designer's recommended tension (number of stitches and rows over a given measurement, see page 22).

lesson 2 | knitting kit

Before you begin any knitting project read the materials section carefully to see what size knitting needles are required and what other equipment, if any, is needed. Here you will find details of the equipment that will form the basis of your knitting workbox and a selection of other equipment that isn't essential but could be useful as you gain experience and move onto more complicated projects.

the essentials

Pairs of knitting needles

Knitting needles come in a wide range of sizes to suit different weights of yarn and a variety of lengths to suit the number of stitches required for a particular project – from 20cm (8in) to 40cm (16in). They are available in various materials from rigid aluminium to flexible bamboo. Metal needles are made mostly from aluminium, though some are made from steel.

These strong materials are particularly suited to small needle sizes. Plastic needles are lightweight and flexible, but can become sticky in humid conditions. Larger-sized needles are made of plastic to reduce their weight. Wood and bamboo needles are lightweight and flexible and virtually silent when knitting. Some knitters find them less tiring to the hands than either plastic or metal.

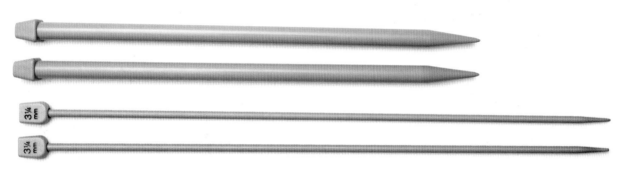

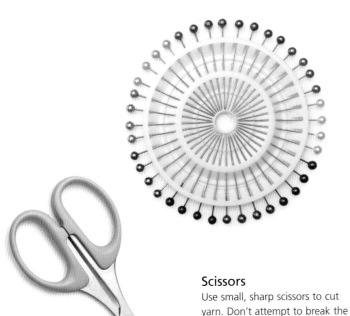

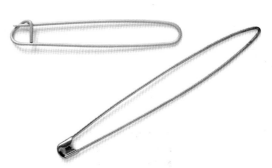

Pins

Long glass-headed pins or knitting pins with a large head are best suited to knitted fabrics – they are easy to see on the knitting and will not get lost in the fabric.

Tapestry needles

A blunt-ended needle with a large eye is required for sewing seams and sewing in ends. They are available in different sizes to suit different weights of yarn; tapestry needles may be used for fine yarns.

Scissors

Use small, sharp scissors to cut yarn. Don't attempt to break the yarn with your fingers as this may result in you cutting your skin.

Stitch holders

These long pins are used for holding groups of stitches until they are required – such as the top of a pocket opening.

Tape measure

These come in various materials, colours and casings – choose one that has clear numbers and is easy to read. A tape measure stretches with use so buy a new one from time to time to ensure accurate measurements.

the extras

Graph/squared paper, pencil and eraser

If you want to design your own cable patterns you'll find it easy to plan and see your design if you chart on graph paper or squared paper. Graph paper with eight or 10 squares to 2.5cm (1in) is a useful size, or you can use a larger-scale squared paper with 5mm (¼in) squares.

Row counters

A row counter can be very useful when working cable patterns to help you keep track of the pattern and the repeats. The barrel type is slipped onto a straight needle and pushed up to the knob. If using large-sized straight needles you will need the clutch type.

Ring markers

These small plastic rings are used to mark a particular place along a row and are slipped from row to row. They are available in various sizes – choose a size that fits loosely over the needles so it is easy to slip from one needle tip to the other.

Split markers

Made from plastic, these split-ring markers are used to mark a particular stitch. They can be added and removed at any time.

Teasel brush

This is a very useful tool when working with fluffy yarns such as mohair. Use it to brush up the surface to enhance the hair (see Hand muff, page 84).

lesson 3 | cable needles

The process of creating cables involves groups of stitches changing places. For this to happen specified stitches must be kept aside so they can be picked up and knitted later to form the cable pattern. Cable needles are simply small double-pointed knitting needles, on which these groups of stitches can be held until they're needed.

Cable needles can be made of simple grey aluminium or steel, coloured plastic or more luxurious polished birch wood or bamboo. Wooden cable needles are often turned so they are slightly slimmer in the centre to help prevent the stitches slipping off, while aluminium and steel ones are a uniform thickness. Alternatively, there are nifty cable needles that have a definite kink in the middle, or are shaped like a large hook, and these avoid all possibility of the stitches slipping off in an unguarded moment.

Cable needles come in a variety of sizes to suit the knitting needles and yarn you are using, and are often sold in sets that include small, medium and large. Extra-large plastic needles are also available for super chunky yarns. Always use a cable needle the same size or slightly smaller than your knitting needles.

Holding stitches

This sample shows cables worked in stocking stitch on a background of reverse stocking stitch. Half the stitches forming the cable (one side of the braid) are slipped onto a straight cable needle and held at the front of the work. Straight needles are best suited to cables that only require 1–4 stitches on the needle. More stitches than this are best held on a kinked needle, to ensure they don't slip off.

use the right cable needle

Cable needles are available in various sizes, shapes, materials and colours. Always use the needle best suited to the stitch and yarn you are using. Cables with more stitches per crossover, or made using thicker yarns, should be held on thicker, more curved cable needles.

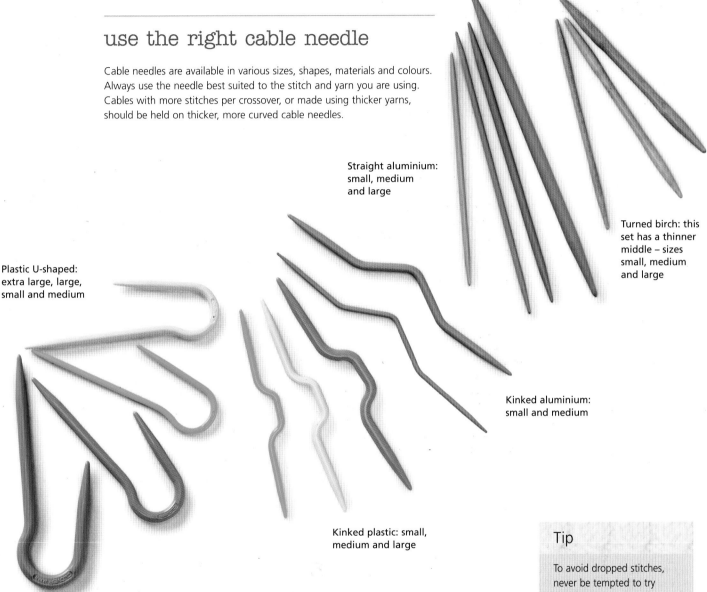

Straight aluminium: small, medium and large

Turned birch: this set has a thinner middle – sizes small, medium and large

Plastic U-shaped: extra large, large, small and medium

Kinked aluminium: small and medium

Kinked plastic: small, medium and large

Tip

To avoid dropped stitches, never be tempted to try cabling without a cable needle, or to use a full size double-pointed needle or crochet hook. To do so will lead to dropped stitches and frustration. Cable needles make things easy, so include them in your knitting kit, use them every time – and enjoy perfect results of what is essentially a simple technique.

Yarn weight	UK knitting needle size	US knitting needle size	Cable needle size
Sport, baby	2.75–3mm	No. 0–2	small
Double knit (DK)	3.25–4mm	No. 3–6	medium
DK, worsted	4.5–5.5mm	No. 7–9	large
Chunky, bulky	6–15mm	No. 10 and above	extra large

knitting basics

Cast on, cast off, knit, purl, stocking stitch, reverse stocking stitch, garter stitch, moss stitch, tension and reading charts – simple steps for perfect results.

lesson 4

casting on

There are several methods of casting on – here we show the thumb method, both English and Continental, and the cable method. These are the most frequently used methods. Unless a pattern states a particular cast on, choose the one you are most comfortable with.

making a slip knot loop

Before you begin your cast on you first need to make a slip knot loop. This is placed on one needle and is counted as the first stitch.

1 Leaving a long end, wind the yarn from the ball around two fingers of your left hand to form a circle.

2 Use one of your knitting needles to pull a loop of yarn from the ball through the circle.

3 Pull the end from the ball of yarn to tighten the loop on the knitting needle. This loop forms your first stitch.

casting on – thumb method (English)

1 Make a slip knot loop onto one needle. Hold the needle with the slip knot loop in your right hand. Gripping the loose end of the yarn in the palm of your left hand, wind the yarn clockwise around your thumb.

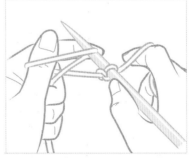

2 Insert the needle into the loop on your thumb from front to back ready to make the next stitch.

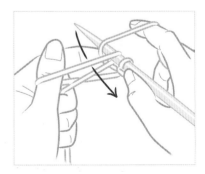

3 Now take the yarn from the ball under the needle and between the needle and your thumb. Draw the needle through the loop and remove your thumb. Pull the end of yarn to tighten the stitch. Continue to cast on stitches in this way.

casting on – thumb method (Continental)

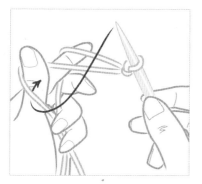 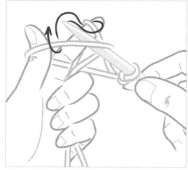 

1 Make a slip knot loop on one needle. Hold the needle with the slip knot loop in your right hand. Take the yarn from the ball over the index finger of your left hand and grip both ends of the yarn in the palm of your left hand, then wind the yarn clockwise around your thumb.

2 Insert the needle under the yarn across the front of your thumb, then under the yarn across your index finger, and pull a loop through the loop on your thumb.

3 Remove your thumb and pull the ends of the yarn to tighten the stitch. Continue to cast on stitches in this way, making sure the stitches are even and move freely on the needle.

casting on – two-needle method or cable cast on

1 Make a slip knot loop, about 12cm (5in) from the end of the yarn. Hold the needle with the slip knot loop in your left hand and insert the right-hand needle into the front of the loop from front to back. Take the yarn from the ball under the right-hand needle and up between the two needles.

2 Draw the right-hand needle back and towards you, pulling the yarn through the slip knot loop to make a new stitch, then transfer the stitch to the left-hand needle.

3 Now insert the right-hand needle between the two stitches on the left-hand needle and take the yarn under the right-hand needle and up between the needles. Draw a loop through and transfer the new stitch to the left-hand needle. Continue to cast on stitches in this way.

lesson 5 | knit and purl

Knit and purl stitch are the two basic knitting stitches and are used in various combinations to make up most stitch patterns. Knit stitch, when used alone, creates a reversible fabric called garter stitch (see overleaf). Alternate rows of knit stitch and purl stitch create a stocking stitch fabric.

knit stitch

The fabric is knitted in rows with each row knitted from right to left, transferring the stitches from the left-hand needle to the right-hand needle. At the end of each row the work is turned, ready to work the next row.

1 Hold the needle with the stitches in your left hand and the yarn from the ball in your right hand. Insert the right-hand needle into the first stitch on the left-hand needle from front to back.

2 Take the yarn under the right-hand needle, between the two needles and over the right-hand needle.

3 With the right-hand needle draw the yarn through the stitch, so forming a new stitch on the right-hand needle. Slip the original stitch off the left-hand needle to complete the first knit stitch. Knit into each stitch in this way until all stitches have been knitted from the left-hand needle onto the right-hand needle.

purl stitch

1 Hold the needle with the stitches in your left hand and the yarn from the ball in your right hand. Insert the right-hand needle into the first stitch on the left-hand needle from back to front.

2 Take the yarn over the right-hand needle, between the two needles and under the right-hand needle.

3 With the right-hand needle draw the yarn through the stitch, so forming a new stitch on the right-hand needle. Slip the original stitch off the left-hand needle to complete the first purl stitch. Purl into each stitch in this way until all stitches have been knitted from the left-hand needle onto the right-hand needle.

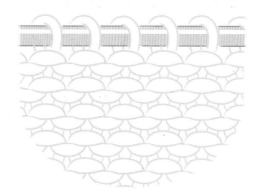

Stocking stitch
By knitting every right-side row and purling every wrong-side row a stocking stitch fabric is produced.

Reverse stocking stitch
By purling every right-side row and knitting every wrong-side row a reverse stocking stitch is produced. This is one of the most commonly used background fabrics worked with cables.

knit and purl through back of the loop

To give a stitch a twisted appearance and make it firmer you can work into the back of the loop.

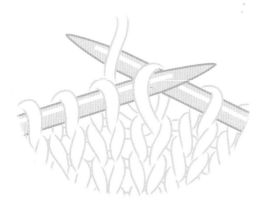

1 To knit through the back of the loop, insert the right-hand needle into the back of the next stitch on the left-hand needle from front to back and knit it in the usual way.

2 To purl through the back of the loop, insert the right-hand needle into the back of the next stitch on the left-hand needle from back to front and purl it in the usual way.

lesson 6 | reversible fabrics

Reversible knitted fabrics include those worked in garter stitch and moss stitch. Both of these stitches work as a background fabric for cables. Alternatively, they can be worked as a simple panel between decorative cable panels.

garter stitch

Garter stitch is a simple, reversible fabric that is formed by working every row in knit stitch. It takes a little longer to 'grow' than stocking stitch because two rows show as only one row.

1 Hold the needle with the stitches in your left hand. Use the right-hand needle to knit the first row – 'V' stitches are formed on the front of the knitting and ridges on the back.

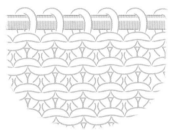

2 Continue to knit every row in this way to produce a garter stitch fabric.

Tip

When using garter stitch in conjunction with cables you will need to block the fabric carefully to open out the length of the garter stitch sections.

moss stitch

Moss stitch is another simple stitch to work and is an ideal fabric to team with cables. It is produced by knitting and purling alternate stitches across a row and knitting purl stitches and purling knit stitches on subsequent rows.

1 Cast on an odd number of stitches and hold the needle with the stitches in your left hand. Use the right-hand needle to knit the first stitch, bring the yarn to the front between the needles, and purl the next stitch.

2 Take the yarn to the back and knit the next stitch. Now purl one stitch then knit one stitch all the way across the row. Each knit stitch will produce a 'V' on the front of the fabric and each purl stitch a ridge.

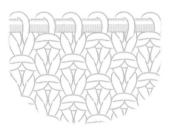

3 On the next row a 'V' (knit stitch) is worked over each ridge and a ridge (purl stitch) over each 'V'. Knit one stitch, then purl one stitch across the row. Continue to work every row in this way to produce a moss stitch fabric.

lesson

casting off

Stitches are cast off to complete your knitting and when a group of stitches is to be decreased – for a buttonhole, an armhole or a neckline. When casting off stitches it is important that an even tension is maintained – neither too tight nor too loose – and that it is elastic. Cast off in the stitch pattern being used, unless stated otherwise.

casting off technique

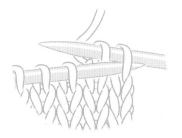

1 When casting off on a knit row, knit the first two stitches so that they are transferred onto the right-hand needle. Insert the left-hand needle, from left to right, into the front of the first stitch on the right-hand needle.

2 Use the left-hand needle to lift the first stitch over the second stitch and off the needle. The first stitch has been cast off and the second stitch remains on the right-hand needle.

3 Knit the next stitch and repeat Step 2 to cast off one stitch. Continue to cast off stitches in this way until one stitch remains on the right-hand needle.

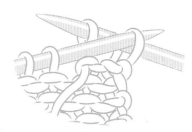

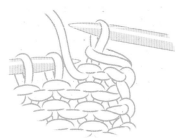

4 To secure the last stitch, cut off the yarn about 10cm (4in) from the knitting and draw the end through the last stitch. Pull the end to tighten.

5 When casting off on a purl row, purl the first two stitches so that they are transferred onto the right-hand needle. Insert the left-hand needle, from left to right, into the front of the first stitch on the right-hand needle.

6 Use the left-hand needle to lift the first stitch over the second stitch and off the needle. Continue to cast off stitches in this way and secure the last stitch, as before.

lesson 8 | tension

Before starting any knitting project it is important that you check your tension – the number of stitches and rows to a centimetre (or inch). The tension achieved by the designer needs to be matched as it determines the measurements of your knitting and ensures you produce an item that is the correct size and shape.

To knit your tension swatch, check the number of stitches and rows required under the heading 'Tension' at the start of each pattern. The tension recommended is chosen to give a correct 'handle' to the work – too tight, and the work will be firm and heavy; too loose, and it will be floppy and open and will tend to lose its shape.

knitting a tension swatch

Stocking stitch has been used in the following steps for clarity.

 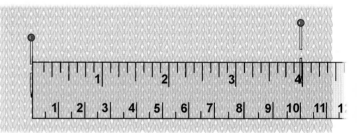

1 Using the correct yarn and needle size for your project, cast on a few more stitches than the number quoted to suit the stitch repeat stated in the tension instructions. Knit the number of rows required plus about 5cm (2in) – this enables you to measure within the cast-on and top edge. Cast off the stitches and block your knitting (see page 128). Lay the knitting, with right side facing, on a flat surface and calculate the number of stitches. Insert a pin centrally on the fabric, a few stitches from the left-hand edge.

2 Place the end of a tape measure in line with the pin and measure across 10cm (4in) and insert another pin. Remove the tape measure and count the number of stitches (including any half stitches). This is the number of stitches to 10cm (4in).

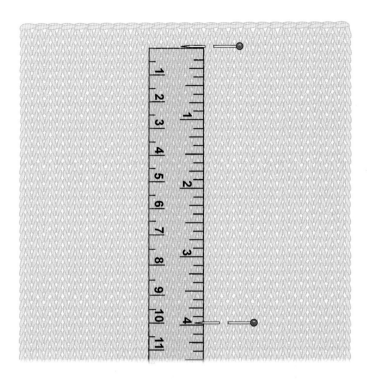

3 To calculate the number of rows, measure 10cm (4in) vertically on a straight line in the centre of the fabric and insert two pins exactly 10cm (4in) apart. Remove the tape measure and count the number of rows between the pins. If your tension matches the recommended tension exactly you are ready to start your project. If not, you will need to adjust your tension (see right).

Tip

You may find it easier to count the number of rows on the reverse side of the knitting – this will depend on the yarn and stitch pattern being used.

adjusting your tension

If your knitting has too many stitches or rows to 10cm (4in), your work is too tight and you need to work on larger needles; too few stitches or rows to 10cm (4in) means your work is too loose and you need to work on smaller needles. Change your needle size accordingly and work another tension swatch. Block the knitting as before and measure the tension (see left). Repeat this process until your tension is exactly right. Remember that a small difference over 10cm (4in) can add up to a big difference over the complete project.

Knitting needle conversion chart

METRIC SIZES (mm)	US SIZES
2.0	0
2.25	1
2.75	2
3.0	–
3.25	3
3.5	4
3.75	5
4.0	6
4.5	7
5.0	8
5.5	9
6.0	10
6.5	10½
7.0	–
7.5	–
8.0	11
9.0	13
10.0	15
12.0	17
16.0	19
19.0	35
25.0	50

lesson 9 | charts

The patterns in this book have been both written and charted. A chart gives a clear visual impression of how the pattern will appear – this can be very useful when placing panels together in a pattern and altering the number of rows in a repeat to make panels work together.

reading charts

Charts are read from the bottom to the top following the direction of the knitting. Each square on the chart represents a stitch and each horizontal line of squares a row of knitting. The symbols represent an instruction and have been designed to resemble the appearance of the knitting.

Before you start knitting familiarize yourself with the symbols on the chart you are going to knit and the techniques involved, making a note of them for quick reference if desired. The symbols and their descriptions can be found on page 140.

rows and repeats

The numbers on each side of the chart indicate the row number, the right- and wrong-side rows and the pattern repeat. The numbers on the right of the chart

indicate the right-side rows and the numbers on the left the wrong-side rows. Check the position of row 1 before you start to knit so that you know whether this is a right- or wrong-side row.

Right-side rows are always read from right to left and wrong-side rows from left to right. Therefore, the symbols on the charts appear from the right side of the work just as they will on the knitting – a knit stitch worked on the wrong side will appear as a ridge on the right side and is shown as a dot (•) on the chart. A blank square represents knit on a right-side row and purl on a wrong-side row.

To keep the pattern repeat correct, not all charts are repeated from row 1. The rows that are to be worked only once to set the pattern, and not repeated, are shaded.

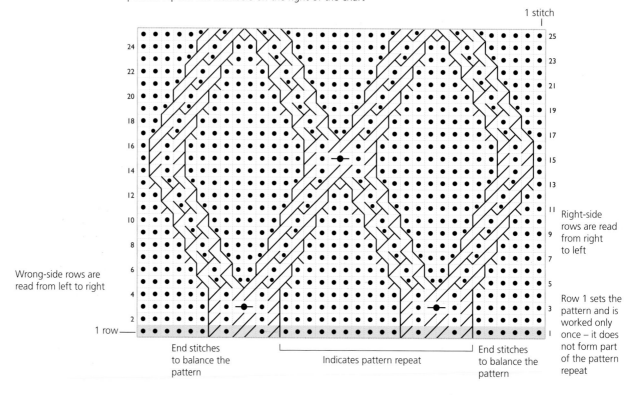

1 stitch

Wrong-side rows are read from left to right

1 row

Right-side rows are read from right to left

Row 1 sets the pattern and is worked only once – it does not form part of the pattern repeat

End stitches to balance the pattern

Indicates pattern repeat

End stitches to balance the pattern

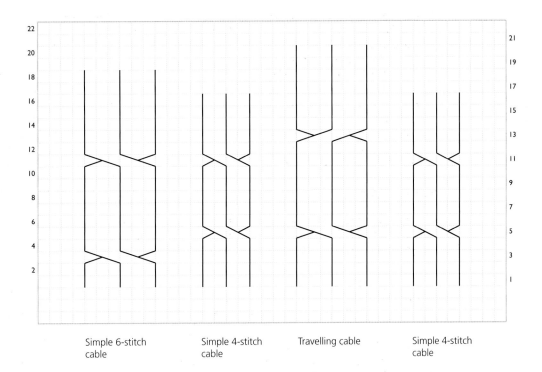

| 22 | | | | 21 |

Simple 6-stitch cable   Simple 4-stitch cable   Travelling cable   Simple 4-stitch cable

positioning cable panels

To work your own combination of cable panels, use a selection of stitch patterns from pages 60–81 and chart the cable designs on squared paper. Leave a few stitches between the panels – these can be filled in later with the stitch to be used for the background fabric. You can adjust the height of most cable panels by adding or subtracting rows – by charting the panels you can see where these adjustments can be made.

Tip

For the seams, allow one stitch at the beginning and end of each row – this will ensure continuity of the pattern and a neat finish.

the cables

Mock cables, cable panels and cable patterns – easy-to-follow stitch patterns and beautiful textured designs in an appealing colour palette.

lesson 10

mock cables

Mock cable techniques produce decorative cable effects but without the use of a separate cable needle to move groups of stitches at the back or front of the work. Instead, the stitches are manipulated at the front of the work in a number of different ways, using only two knitting needles to create raised designs that mimic real cable.

Two simple techniques – slipping and binding – enable the stitches to travel across the knitted fabric, while an attractive wrapping technique gathers groups of stitches together. Used alone, each technique creates a range of fascinating designs. Used in combination they offer endless possibilities for intriguingly textured surface patterns. The effects are just as intricate and beautiful as real cable, but mock cable patterns have the advantage of being quicker to work.

As with real cable, mock cable patterns are most often worked against a plain background – generally reverse stocking stitch – to highlight the designs, and they can be worked in any yarn. Fine yarns create delicately detailed patterns for sweaters and wraps, while heavier yarns produce boldly textured fabrics for chunky jackets and up-to-the-minute home furnishings.

Mock cables can be used in a repeat design of textured panels or bands or to create focus in particular areas of a garment. They can be combined with real cables and other raised designs for yet more decorative texturing options.

Practice pattern
Use this pattern to work through the step-by-step exercise overleaf to make the sample as shown.

Pattern

Row 1 (RS) P2, *K3, P2, rep from * to end.
Row 2 K2, *P3, K2, rep from * to end.
Row 3 P2, *B3, P2, rep from * to end.
Row 4 As row 2.
These 4 rows form the patt.

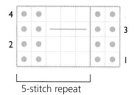

5-stitch repeat

slip stitch cable

This sample shows six pattern repeats. Worked on a multiple of 5 stitches plus 2.

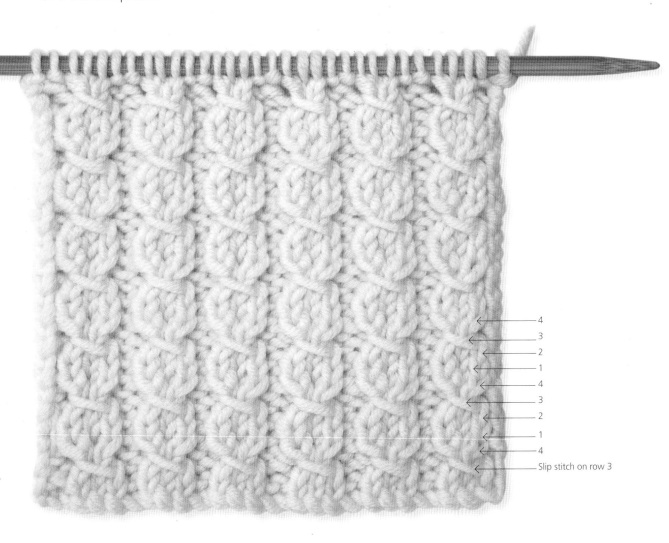

← 4
← 3
← 2
← 1
← 4
← 3
← 2
← 1
← 4
← Slip stitch on row 3

5mm
(Size 8)

Aran

binding stitches

width of mock cable

1 Stitches are bound by passing a stitch across a given group of stitches – on this pattern three stitches are bound with one stitch. On rows 1 and 2 the width of the mock cable is set – here the width is three stitches with two background stitches worked between.

slipped stitch

2 On row 3 the stitches are bound – this is referred to as Bind 3 (abbreviated as B3) in the instructions. With the yarn at the back of the knitting, the first stitch of the group is slipped purlwise – keeping the yarn at the back avoids a strand of yarn across the front of the knitting and slipping the stitch purlwise keeps the stitch straight.

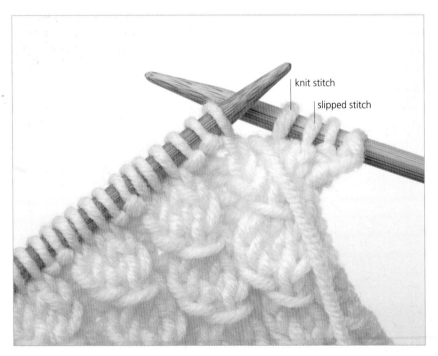

knit stitch

slipped stitch

3 The slipped stitch is used to bind the stitches. Before this process can be worked an extra stitch needs to be made to compensate for the slipped stitch that will be removed from the needle. Knit the next stitch, then bring the yarn to the front between the needles.

yarn across needle

4 Take the yarn from the front across the right-hand needle and to the back so that it is in position to knit the next stitch. The yarn lying across the right-hand needle makes a stitch. Knit the next stitch in the usual way.

5 Now bind the stitches with the slipped stitch. Insert the point of the left-hand needle into the slipped stitch from left to right. Pass the slipped stitch over (abbreviated as psso) the first knitted stitch, the new stitch and the next knitted stitch. This completes the Bind 3 (B3) and forms the first mock cable.

6 By binding each group of three stitches mock cables are formed across the row. Here the mock cable is formed every four rows.

corded cable

This sample shows four pattern repeats. Worked on a multiple of 6 stitches plus 4.

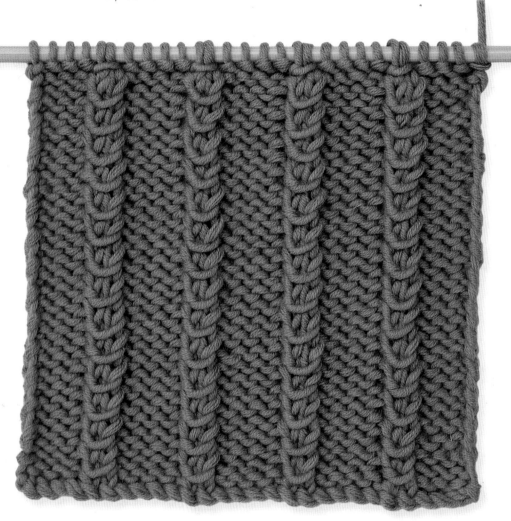

3.75mm
(Size 5)

DK cotton

Pattern

Row 1 (RS) P4, *K2, P4, rep from * to end.
Row 2 K4, *B2, K4, rep from * to end.
These 2 rows form the patt.

6-stitch repeat

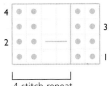

variation

Worked on a multiple of
4 stitches plus 2.

3.75mm
(Size 5)

DK cotton

Pattern

Row 1 (RS) P2, *K2, P2, rep from * to end.
Row 2 K2, *B2, K2, rep from * to end.
Row 3 As row 1.
Row 4 K2, *P2, K2, rep from * to end.
These 4 rows form the patt.

```
4 ● ● | ● ● 
  ● ● | ● ●  3
2 ● ● |—— ● ●
  ● ● | ● ●  1
```
4-stitch repeat

eyelet cable

This sample shows seven pattern repeats. Worked on a multiple of 5 stitches plus 2.

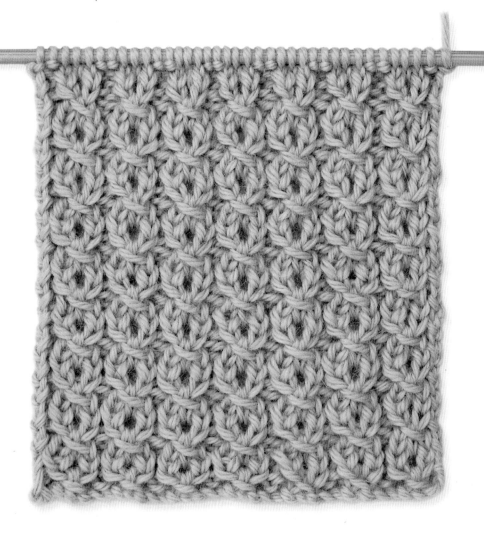

3.75mm
(Size 5)

DK Alpaca

Pattern

Row 1 (RS) P2, *sl 1 purlwise with yarn at back, K2, psso the 2 knit sts, P2, rep from * to end.
Row 2 K2, *P1, yrn, P1, K2, rep from * to end.
Row 3 P2, *K3, P2, rep from * to end.
Row 4 K2, *P3, K2, rep from * to end.
These 4 rows form the patt.

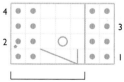

5-stitch repeat

variation

Worked on a multiple of
5 stitches plus 2.

5mm
(Size 8)

Fine
mohair

Lacy look
Worked in a fine mohair yarn
on 5mm (size 8) knitting needles,
the eyelet cable pattern has a
delicate, lacy appearance.

slip stitch braid

This sample shows four pattern repeats. Worked on a multiple of 8 stitches plus 4.

X 4mm (Size 6)

DK wool

Pattern

Row 1 (WS) K4, *P4, K4, rep from * to end.
Row 2 P4, *(Br2) twice, P4, rep from * to end.
Row 3 As row 1.
Row 4 P4, *K1, Br2, K1, P4, rep from * to end.
These 4 rows form the patt.

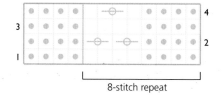

8-stitch repeat

variation

Worked on a multiple of
8 stitches plus 4.

5mm
(Size 8)

Aran

Pattern

Row 1 (WS) K4, *P4, K4, rep from * to end.
Row 2 P4, *(Br2) twice, P4, rep from * to end.
Row 3 As row 1.
Row 4 P4, *K1, Br2, K1, P4, rep from * to end.
Row 5 As row 1.
Row 6 As row 4.
These 6 rows form the patt.

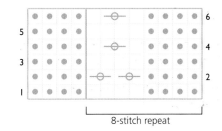

8-stitch repeat

slipped braid cable

This sample shows four pattern repeats.
Worked on a multiple of 8 stitches plus 3.

3.75mm
(Size 5)

DK Alpaca

Pattern

Row 1 (WS) K3, *P5, K3, rep from *
to end.
Row 2 P3, *K2, sl 1 purlwise with yarn
at back, K2, P3, rep from * to end.
Row 3 K3, *P2, sl 1 with yarn at front,
P2, K3, rep from * to end.
Row 4 P3, *K2, drop slipped st to front
of work, K2, pick up dropped st and K
it, P3, rep from * to end.

Rows 5 to 7 As rows 1 to 3.
Row 8 P3, *sl 2, drop next slipped st to
front of work, then slip the same 2 sts
back onto LH needle, pick up dropped
st and K it, K4, P3, rep from * to end.
These 8 rows form the patt.

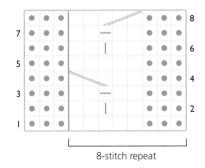

8-stitch repeat

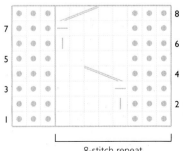

variation

Worked on a multiple of
8 stitches plus 3.

3.75mm
(Size 5)

DK Alpaca

Pattern

Row 1 (WS) K3, *P5, K3, rep from * to end.
Row 2 P3, *sl 1 purlwise with yarn at back, K4, P3, rep from * to end.
Row 3 K3, *P4, sl 1 with yarn at front, K3, rep from * to end.
Row 4 P3, *drop slipped st to front of work, K2, pick up dropped st and K it, K2, P3, rep from * to end.
Row 5 As row 1.

Row 6 P3, *K4, sl 1 purlwise with yarn at back, P3, rep from * to end.
Row 7 K3, *sl 1 with yarn at front, P4, K3, rep from * to end.
Row 8 P3, *K2, sl 2, drop next slipped st to front of work, then slip the same 2 sts back onto LH needle, pick up dropped st and K it, K2, P3, rep from * to end.
These 8 rows form the patt.

8-stitch repeat

oblique cable

This sample shows three pattern repeats. Worked on a multiple of 8 stitches plus 1.

5mm
(Size 8)

DK wool

Pattern

Row 1 (WS) P to end.
Row 2 P1, *K3, P1, Cr3, P1, rep from * to end.
Row 3 P to end.
Row 4 P1, *Cr3, P1, K3, P1, rep from * to end.
These 4 rows form the patt.

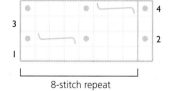

8-stitch repeat

variation

Worked on a multiple of
17 stitches plus 6.

5mm
(Size 8)

DK wool

Pattern

Row 1 (WS) P to end.
Row 2 P6, *K3, P1, Cr3, P1, K3, P6,
rep from * to end.
Row 3 P to end.
Row 4 P6 *Cr3, P1, K3, P1, Cr3, P6,
rep from * to end.
These 4 rows form the patt.

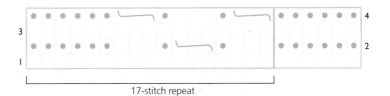

17-stitch repeat

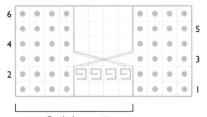

cross stitch cable

This sample shows four pattern repeats. Worked on a multiple of 8 stitches plus 4.

 4mm
(Size 6)

 DK

Pattern

Row 1 (RS) P4, *K4, P4, rep from * to end.
Row 2 K4, *P4 wrapping yarn twice around needle for each st, K4, rep from * to end.
Row 3 P4, *Cr4, P4, rep from * to end.
Row 4 K4, *P4, K4, rep from * to end.
Row 5 As row 1.
Row 6 As row 4.
These 6 rows form the patt.

8-stitch repeat

variation

Worked on a multiple of
10 stitches plus 4.

5mm
(Size 8)

Aran tweed

Pattern

Row 1 (RS) P4, *K6, P4, rep from * to end.
Row 2 K4, *P6 wrapping yarn twice around
needle for each st, K4, rep from * to end.
Row 3 P4, *Cr6, P4, rep from * to end.
Row 4 K4, *P6, K4, rep from * to end.
Row 5 As row 1.
Row 6 As row 4
Row 7 As row 1.
Row 8 As row 4.
These 8 rows form the patt.

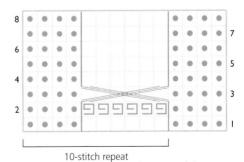

10-stitch repeat

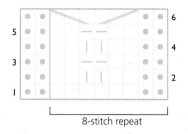

mock gull stitch

This sample shows four pattern repeats. Worked on a multiple of 8 stitches plus 2.

3.75mm
(Size 5)

DK

Pattern

Row 1 (WS) K2, *P6, K2, rep from * to end.

Row 2 P2, *K2, sl 2 purlwise with yarn at back, K2, P2, rep from * to end.

Row 3 K2, *p2, sl 2 with yarn at front, P2, K2, rep from * to end.

Rows 4 and 5 As rows 2 and 3.

Row 6 P2, *sl 2, drop next slipped st to front of work, slip the same 2 sts back onto LH needle, pick up dropped st and K it, then K2, drop next slipped st to front of work, K2, pick up dropped st and K it, P2, rep from * to end.
These 6 rows form the patt.

8-stitch repeat

variation

Worked on a multiple of
8 stitches plus 2.

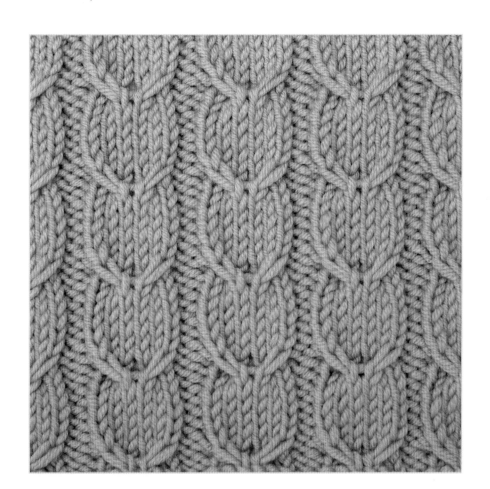

5mm
(Size 8)

Aran

Pattern

Row 1 (WS) K2, *P6, K2, rep from *
to end.
Row 2 P2, *K2, sl 2 purlwise with yarn
at back, K2, P2, rep from * to end.
Row 3 K2, *p2, sl 2 with yarn at front,
P2, K2, rep from * to end.
Row 4 P2, *sl 2, drop next slipped st to
front of work, slip the same 2 sts back
onto LH needle, pick up dropped st and

K it, then K2, drop next slipped st to
front of work, K2, pick up dropped st
and K it, P2, rep from * to end.
Row 5 As row 1.
Row 6 P2, *K6, P2, rep from * to end.
Row 7 As row 1.
Row 8 As row 6.
These 8 rows form the patt.

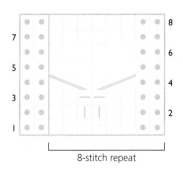

8-stitch repeat

smocked cable

This sample shows two pattern repeats.
Worked on a multiple of 16 stitches
plus 6.

4mm
(Size 6)

DK Alpaca

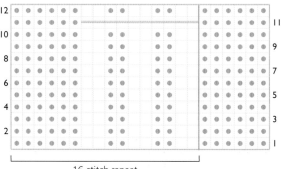

Pattern

Row 1 (RS) P6, *K2, (P2, K2) twice, P6, rep
from * to end.
Row 2 K6, *P2, (K2, P2) twice, K6, rep from *
to end.
Rows 3 to 10 Work rows 1 and 2 four times.
Row 11 P6, *W10, P6, rep from * to end.
Row 12 As row 2.
These 12 rows form the patt.

variation

Worked on a multiple of
30 stitches plus 20.

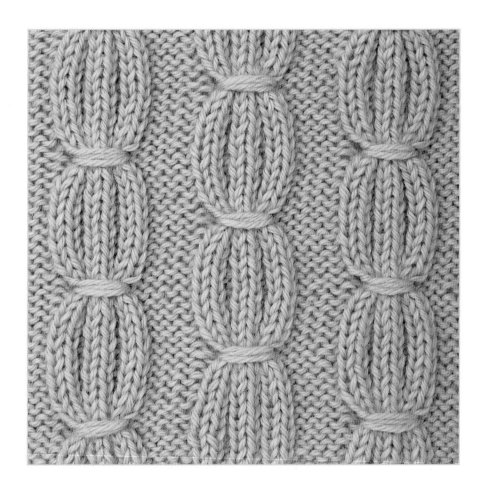

4mm
(Size 6)

DK Alpaca

Pattern

Row 1 (RS) P5, *K2, (P2, K2) twice, P5, rep from * to end.
Row 2 K5, *P2, (K2, P2) twice, K5, rep from * to end.
Rows 3 and 4 As rows 1 and 2.
Row 5 P5, W10, P5, *K2, (P2, K2) twice, P5, W10, P5, rep from * to end.
Row 6 As row 2.
Rows 7 to 10 Work rows 1 and 2 twice.
Row 11 P5, K2, (P2, K2) twice, P5, *W10, P5, K2, (P2, K2) twice, P5, rep from * to end.
Row 12 As row 2.
These 12 rows form the patt.

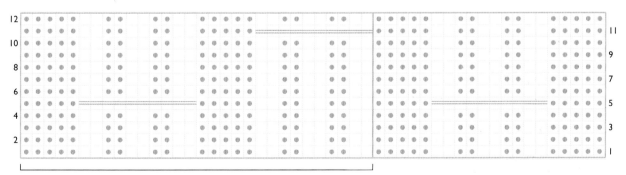

30-stitch repeat

slipped circular cable

This sample shows four pattern repeats. Worked on a multiple of 9 stitches plus 2.

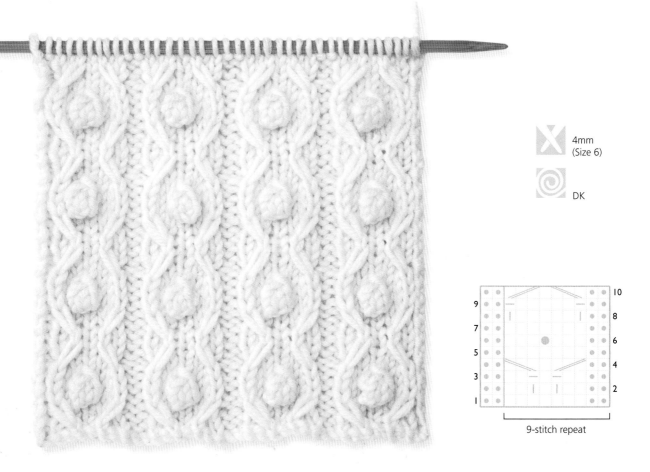

4mm
(Size 6)

DK

9-stitch repeat

Pattern

Row 1 (WS) K2, *P7, K2, rep from * to end.

Row 2 P2, *K2, sl 1 purlwise with yarn at back, K1, sl 1 purlwise with yarn at back, K2, P2, rep from * to end.

Row 3 K2, *P2, sl 1 purlwise with yarn at front, P1, sl 1 purlwise with yarn at front, P2, K2, rep from * to end.

Row 4 P2, *sl 2, drop next slipped st to front of work, slip the same 2 sts back onto LH needle, pick up dropped st and K it, K3, then drop next slipped st to front of work, K2, pick up dropped st and K it, P2, rep from * to end.

Row 5 As row 1.

Row 6 P2, *K3, MB-1, K3, P2, rep from * to end.

Row 7 As row 1.

Row 8 P2, *sl 1 purlwise with yarn at back, K5, sl 1 purlwise with yarn at back, P2, rep from * to end.

Row 9 K2, *sl 1 purlwise with yarn at front, P5, sl 1 purlwise with yarn at front, K2, rep from * to end.

Row 10 P2, *drop slipped st to front of work, K2, pick up dropped st and K it, K1, sl 2, drop next slipped st to front of work, slip the same 2 sts back onto LH needle, pick up dropped st and K it, K2, P2, rep from * to end.

These 10 rows form the patt.

variation

Worked on a multiple of
9 stitches plus 2.

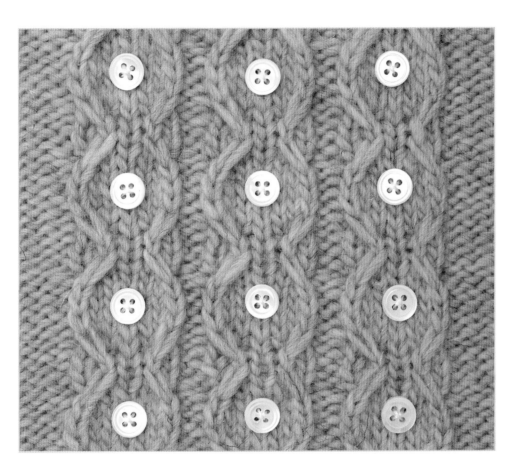

5mm
(Size 8)

DK wool

Buttons instead of bobbles
The ten pattern rows have been worked omitting
the bobbles. A small mother-of-pearl button has
been added to the centre of each pattern.

project 1: mug and tea cosies

A modern take on traditional designs, these stylish cosies are knitted in DK yarn using a simple slip stitch pattern that has elasticity – so creating a snug fit.

Mug cosy pattern

TO MAKE (made in one piece)
Using 4mm (size 6) needles cast on 57 sts.
Work in Slip Stitch Cable patt as follows:
Row 1 (RS) P2, *K3, P2, rep from * to end.
Row 2 K2, *P3, K2, rep from * to end.
Row 3 P2, *B3, P2, rep from * to end.
Row 4 As row 2.
These 4 rows form the patt.
Rep them 3 times more. Cast off in patt.

mug cosy

YOU WILL NEED
- 10g DK yarn in natural for each cosy
- 4mm (size 6) knitting needles
- Crochet hook or hairpin
- Mugs

SIZE
19 x 5cm (7½ x 2in)
To fit a mug with a circumference of 22cm (8½in) and a base handle height of no less than 1.5cm (½in)

TENSION
30 sts and 32 rows to 10cm (4in) over patt, with patt slightly opened out

TIES (make 4)

Using two 1m (1yd) lengths of yarn make a twisted cord (see page 134), tying a knot with the loose ends only. Trim the ends. Insert a crochet hook or the loop of a hairpin into one corner of the mug cosy, from back to front, and use to pull the folded end of one twisted cord through the knitting. Ease open the folded end, pull the knotted end through and draw up close to the knitting. Attach a tie to each corner in this way. Place the cosy around the mug and form the ties into bows to secure in place.

Tea cosy pattern

BACK AND FRONT (alike)
Using 4mm (size 6) needles cast on 52 sts.
Work in Slip Stitch Cable patt as follows:
Row 1 (RS) P2, *K3, P2, rep from * to end.
Row 2 K2, *P3, K2, rep from * to end.
Row 3 P2, *B3, P2, rep from * to end.
Row 4 As row 2.
These 4 rows form the patt.
Cont in patt until work measures 15cm (6in)
from beg, ending row 3.
(Length can be adjusted here.)
Next row K2 tog, *P1, K1, P1, K2 tog, rep
from * to end. 41 sts.
Now work ribbed band as follows:
Next row P1, *K1, P1, rep from * to end.
Next row K1, *P1, K1, rep from * to end.
Rep last 2 rows twice more.
Cast off knitwise.

tea cosy

YOU WILL NEED
• 100g DK yarn in natural
• 4mm (size 6) knitting needles
• 2 buttons

SIZE
To fit a teapot with a circumference of 38cm (15in)
and a height of 11cm (4½in) to lid (adjustable)

TENSION
30 sts and 32 rows to 10cm (4in) over patt, with
patt slightly opened out

TO FINISH
Block back and front to size. Pin the side seams
leaving a gap for the handle and spout. Place the
cosy over the teapot and adjust the openings if
necessary. Carefully remove the cosy and join the
side seams. Press seams lightly using a warm iron
over a damp cloth.

Using three 3m (3yd) lengths of yarn make a
twisted cord (see page 134). Starting at the centre
front, thread the cord evenly around the cosy just
below the ribbed band.

Place the cosy over the teapot and draw up the
cord around the knob on the lid. Secure with a bow.
Knot and trim the ends for length required. Sew a
button to each end of the cord for decoration.

project 2: placemat and napkin ring

This chic table set is knitted in practical cotton. The placemat has an integral pocket to hold your cutlery and the napkin ring is trimmed with shiny beads.

designer's tip

To work W10 with beads, push six beads up close to the knitting before wrapping the yarn around the group of stitches. Wrap the yarn anticlockwise, twice around the stitches to gather them, placing six beads on the front of the knitting with each wrap.

YOU WILL NEED

• 150g DK cotton for each placemat and napkin ring set
• 4mm (size 6) knitting needles
• 48 size 6/0 Rocaille beads in grey lustre for each napkin ring

SIZE

Placemat 33 x 46cm (13 x 18in)
Napkin ring 7cm (3in) wide x 9cm (3½in) diameter

TENSION

20 sts and 32 rows to 10cm (4in) over Moss st

TO FINISH

Block knitting to size. Sew down pocket lining. Sew in the ends.

Placemat pattern

POCKET LINING

Using 4mm (size 6) needles cast on 27 sts.
Row 1 (RS) (P2, K2) 3 times, P3, (K2, P2) 3 times.
Row 2 (K2, P2) 3 times, K3, (P2, K2) 3 times.
Rep these 2 rows 18 times more.
Cut off yarn and leave sts on a holder.

MAIN PIECE

Using 4mm (size 6) needles cast on 91 sts.
Moss st row K1, *P1, K1, rep from * to end.
Rep this row 4 times more.
Next row Patt 66, work into front and back of next 5 sts, patt 3, work into front and back of next 5 sts, patt to end. 101 sts.
Now work in Moss st with Smocked Cable panel as follows:
Row 1 (RS) Patt 10, (P2, K2) 3 times, P3, (K2, P2) 3 times, patt to end.
Row 2 Patt 64, (K2, P2) 3 times, K3, (P2, K2) 3 times, patt to end.

Rows 3 to 10 Work rows 1 and 2 four times.
Row 11 Patt 10, P2, W10, P3, W10, P2, patt to end.
Row 12 As row 2.
These 12 rows form the patt.
Rep them twice more, then work the first 2 rows again.
Next row Patt 10, P2, K2 tog, (P2 tog, K2 tog) twice, P3, K2 tog, (P2 tog, K2 tog) twice, P2, patt to end. 91 sts.
Pocket row 1 Patt 64, cast off 17 purlwise, patt to end.
Pocket row 2 Patt 10, patt across sts of pocket lining, patt to end. 101 sts.
Cont in Moss st patt with cable panel until row 7 of the 8th patt has been worked.
Next row Patt 66, P2 tog, (K2 tog, P2 tog) twice, K3, P2 tog, (K2 tog, P2 tog) twice, patt to end. 91 sts.
Now work the Moss st row 5 times.
Cast off.

Napkin ring pattern

TO MAKE

Thread 48 beads onto a ball of yarn. Push the beads along the yarn until you are ready to work with them.

Using the same ball of yarn and 4mm (size 6) needles cast on 18 sts.

Work in Smocked Cable patt with Moss st edging as follows:

Row 1 (RS) P1, K1, P2 *K2, P2, rep from * to last 2 sts, K1, P1.

Row 2 P1, K3, (P2, K2) to last 2 sts, K1, P1.

Rows 3 to 6 Work rows 1 and 2 twice.

Row 7 P1, K1, P2, push 12 beads along the yarn and work W10 but wind the yarn twice around the sts placing six beads on the front of the knitting (see designer's tip), then P2, K1, P1.

Row 8 As row 2.

Rows 9 to 12 Work rows 1 and 2 twice. These 12 rows form the patt.

Rep them 3 times more. Cast off.

TO FINISH

Block knitting to size. With right sides together, join the short edges. Turn to the right side.

project 3: scarf

Knit a luxurious scarf in a blend of alpaca and silk.
Wear it loose or fasten it with a large decorative pin.

Pattern

TO MAKE

Using 5.5mm (size 9) needles and A, cast
on 44 sts.
Work in Cross Stitch Cable patt as follows:
Row 1 (RS) P4, *K6, P4, rep from * to end.
Row 2 K4, *P6 wrapping yarn twice around
needle for each st, K4, rep from * to end.
Row 3 P4, *Cr6, P4, rep from * to end.
Row 4 K4, *P6, K4, rep from * to end.
Row 5 As row 1.
Row 6 As row 4.
Row 7 As row 1.
Row 8 As row 4.
These 8 rows form the patt.
Cont in patt, working in stripes of 16 rows A,
16 rows B and 16 rows C until the fifth stripe
in B has been worked.
Cont with B, work 4 more rows. Cast off.

YOU WILL NEED

• 100g Aran yarn in each of cream
(A), stone (B) and fawn (C)
• 5.5mm (size 9) knitting needles
• Large decorative pin to fasten
(optional)

SIZE

18cm (7in) wide by 135cm (53in) long

TENSION

1 patt rep of 10 sts to 4cm (1½in)
and 16 rows to 8cm (3¼in) over cable
patt, with patt slightly opened out

TO FINISH

Block knitting to size. Sew in the ends.

designer's tip

When changing colour, loosely tie the two
colours together at the beginning of the row
close to the needle. Cut off the previous colour
leaving an end about 10cm (4in) long. Continue
knitting with the new colour. When you have
completed your knitting, untie the loose knot and
use a tapestry needle to weave the ends neatly
into the back of the knitting.

project 4: storage basket

A functional basket knitted in a simple braided stitch pattern and crisp cotton for texture and stability.

Pattern

SHORT SIDES (make 2)
Using 3.75mm (size 5) needles cast on 36 sts.
Work in Slip Stitch Braid patt as follows:
Row 1 (WS) K4, *P4, K4, rep from * to end.
Row 2 P4, *(Br2) twice, P4, rep from * to end.
Row 3 As row 1.
Row 4 P4, *K1, Br2, K1, P4, rep from * to end.
These 4 rows form the patt.
Cont in patt until work measures 11cm (4½in) from beg, ending row 1.
Now work cuff as follows:
Beg row 1 to reverse patt, work 14 rows.
Cast off.

LONG SIDES (make 2)
Using 3.75mm (size 5) needles cast on 60 sts.
Work as given for short sides.

BASE
Using 3.75mm (size 5) needles cast on 36 sts.
Beg with a P row, work in rev st st until work measures 25cm (10in) from beg, ending with a K row. Cast off.

YOU WILL NEED
- 150g DK cotton in brown
- 3.75mm (size 5) knitting needles
- Laundry starch powder (optional)

SIZE
15 x 25cm (6 x 10in)
Height 11cm (4½in) with cuff turned back

TENSION
24 sts and 36 rows to 10cm (4in) over patt
26 sts and 32 rows to 10cm (4in) over st st

TO FINISH
Block pieces to size. With WS together, pin a short side to each end of the long sides. Join the seams neatly (see designer's tip), reversing the seam on the cuff section. With WS together pin the base to the side sections, placing a corner at each side seam. Join the seams. Press the seams lightly with a warm iron over a damp cloth. To stiffen the fabric, rinse the basket in a solution of laundry starch powder following the manufacturer's instructions.

designer's tip

For a neat, straight seam, join the side sections together with mattress stitch – see page 130. Then use mattress stitch to sew the base in position, joining the row-ends of the base to the cast-on stitches of the long sides.

working a simple cable

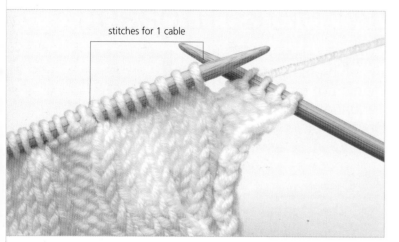

stitches for 1 cable

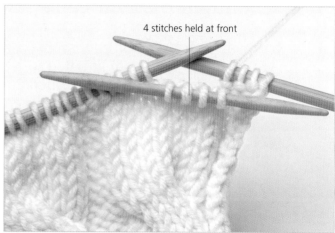

4 stitches held at front

1 A cable is formed by changing the formation of a group of stitches, by moving one group of stitches over another with the help of a cable needle. On a right-side row, work to the position of the cable.

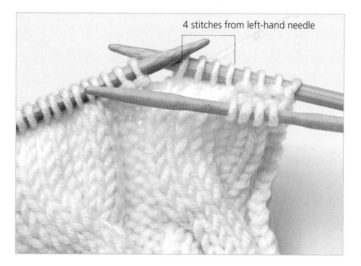

4 stitches from left-hand needle

2 To work an 8-stitch cable that slants to the left, the stitches on the cable needle are held at the front of the work. Slip the next four stitches onto a cable needle and leave at the front of the work (abbreviated as C8F).

3 Knit the next four stitches on the left-hand needle – the remaining four stitches of the cable. The four stitches on the cable needle remain at the front.

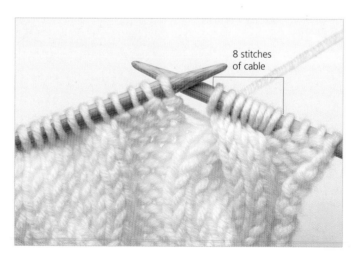

8 stitches of cable

4 Now knit the four stitches from the cable needle to produce the crossover. If you have difficulty knitting the stitches from the cable needle, slip them back onto the left-hand needle and knit them in the usual way. The eight stitches of the cable are now on the right-hand needle.

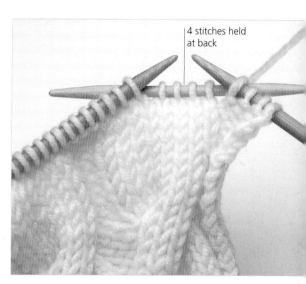

5 By working a cable (C8F) at regular intervals – for this pattern it is on every tenth row – a rope effect is produced, with each cable slanting to the left.

6 To work an 8-stitch cable that slants to the right, the stitches on the cable needle are held at the back of the work. On a right-side row, work to the position of the cable. Slip the next four stitches onto a cable needle and leave at the back of the work (abbreviated as C8B).

4 stitches held at back

8 stitches of cable

7 Knit the next four stitches on the left-hand needle, then knit the four stitches from the cable needle. By working a cable (C8B) at regular intervals – for this pattern it is on every tenth row – a rope effect is produced with each cable slanting to the right.

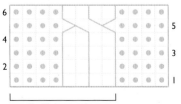

simple 4-stitch cable

This sample shows four cable panels with 4 stitches worked in reverse stocking stitch between.
Worked on a multiple of 8 stitches plus 4.

⊠ 4.5mm (Size 7)

◎ DK wool

Single panel

Row 1 (RS) K4.
Row 2 P4.
Rows 3 and 4 As rows 1 and 2.
Row 5 C4F.
Row 6 As row 2.
These 6 rows form the patt.

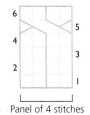

To cross the stitches to the right work C4B on row 5, as shown at left.

Panel of 4 stitches

Pattern

Row 1 (RS) P4, *K4, P4, rep from * to end.
Row 2 K4, *P4, K4, rep from * to end.
Rows 3 and 4 As rows 1 and 2.
Row 5 P4, *C4F, P4, rep from * to end.
Row 6 As row 2.
These 6 rows form the patt.

8-stitch repeat

simple 6-stitch cable

This sample shows three cable panels with
4 stitches worked in reverse stocking stitch between.
Worked on a multiple of 10 stitches plus 4.

4.5mm
(Size 7)

DK wool

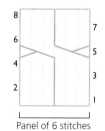

Single panel

Row 1 (RS) K6.
Row 2 P6.
Rows 3 and 4 As rows 1 and 2.
Row 5 C6F.
Row 6 As row 2.
Rows 7 and 8 As rows 1 and 2.
These 8 rows form the patt.

To cross the stitches to the
right work C6B on row 5, as
shown at left.

Panel of 6 stitches

Pattern

Row 1 (RS) P4, *K6, P4, rep from * to end.
Row 2 K4, *P6, K4, rep from * to end.
Rows 3 and 4 As rows 1 and 2.
Row 5 P4, *C6F, P4, rep from * to end.
Row 6 As row 2.
Rows 7 and 8 As rows 1 and 2.
These 8 rows form the patt.

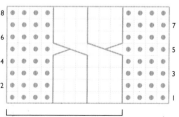

10-stitch repeat

twisted rib cable

This sample shows three cable panels with 3 stitches worked in reverse stocking stitch between. Worked on a multiple of 10 stitches plus 3.

3.75mm
(Size 5)

DK Alpaca

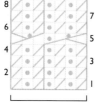

Single panel

Row 1 (RS) K1tbl, (P1, K1tbl) 3 times.
Row 2 P1tbl, (K1, P1tbl) 3 times.
Rows 3 and 4 As rows 1 and 2.
Row 5 C7B rib.
Row 6 As row 2.
Rows 7 and 8 As rows 1 and 2.
These 8 rows form the patt.

Panel of 7 stitches

Pattern

Row 1 (RS) P3, *K1tbl, (P1, K1tbl) 3 times, P3, rep from * to end.
Row 2 K3, *P1tbl, (K1, P1tbl) 3 times, K3, rep from * to end.
Rows 3 and 4 As rows 1 and 2.
Row 5 P3, *C7B rib, P3, rep from * to end.
Row 6 As row 2.
Rows 7 and 8 As rows 1 and 2.
These 8 rows form the patt.

10-stitch repeat

variation

Worked on a multiple
of 10 stitches plus 3.

 5mm
(Size 8)

 Aran

Single panel

Row 1 (RS) K1tbl, (P1,
K1tbl) 3 times.
Row 2 P1tbl, (K1, P1tbl)
3 times.
Rows 3 and 4 As rows
1 and 2.
Row 5 C7B rib.
Row 6 As row 2.
Rows 7 to 12 Work rows
1 and 2 three times.
These 12 rows form the patt.

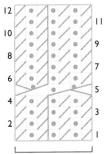

Panel of 7 stitches

Pattern

Row 1 (RS) P3, *K1tbl, (P1, K1tbl)
3 times, P3, rep from * to end.
Row 2 K3, *P1tbl, (K1, P1tbl) 3 times,
K3, rep from * to end.
Rows 3 and 4 As rows 1 and 2.
Row 5 P3, *C7B rib, P3, rep from *
to end.
Row 6 As row 2.
Rows 7 to 12 Work rows 1 and 2
three times.
These 12 rows form the patt.

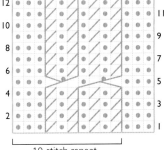

10-stitch repeat

cable and braid

This sample shows four pattern repeats.
Worked on a multiple of 9 stitches plus 5.

3.75mm
(Size 5)

DK Alpaca

Single panel

Row 1 (RS) K1tbl, P2, K4, P2, K1tbl.
Row 2 P1tbl, K2, P4, K2, P1tbl.
Row 3 K1tbl, P2, C4B, P2, K1tbl.
Row 4 As row 2.
Rows 5 and 6 As rows 1 and 2.
These 6 rows form the patt.

Pattern

Row 1 (RS) P2, K1tbl, P2, *K4, P2, K1tbl, P2,
rep from * to end.
Row 2 K2, P1tbl, K2, *P4, K2, P1tbl, K2, rep
from * to end.
Row 3 P2, K1tbl, P2, *C4B, P2, K1tbl, P2, rep
from * to end.
Row 4 As row 2.
Rows 5 and 6 As rows 1 and 2.
These 6 rows form the patt.

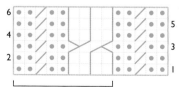

Panel of 10 stitches

9-stitch repeat

variation

Worked on a multiple
of 9 stitches plus 5.

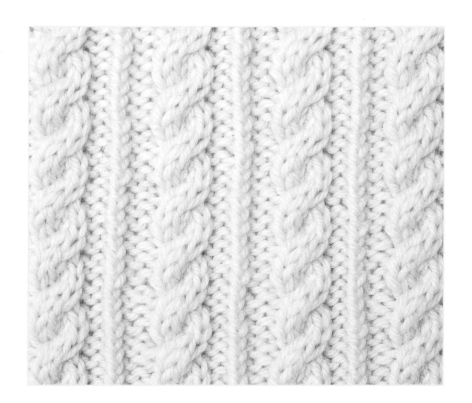

5mm
(Size 8)

Aran

Single panel

Row 1 (RS) K1tbl, P2, K4, P2, K1tbl.
Row 2 P1tbl, K2, P4, K2, P1tbl.
Row 3 K1tbl, P2, C4B, P2, K1tbl.
Row 4 As row 2.
These 4 rows form the patt.

Pattern

Row 1 (RS) P2, K1tbl, P2, *K4, P2, K1tbl, P2,
rep from * to end.
Row 2 K2, P1tbl, K2, *P4, K2, P1tbl, K2, rep
from * to end.
Row 3 P2, K1tbl, P2, *C4B, P2, K1tbl, P2, rep
from * to end.
Row 4 As row 2.
These 4 rows form the patt.

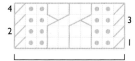

Panel of 10 stitches

9-stitch repeat

plaited cable

This sample shows three cable panels with 4 stitches worked in reverse stocking stitch between. Worked on a multiple of 13 stitches plus 4.

3.75mm
(Size 5)

DK Alpaca

Single panel

Row 1 (RS) K9.
Row 2 P9.
Row 3 K3, C6F.
Row 4 As row 2.
Rows 5 and 6 As rows 1 and 2.
Row 7 C6B, K3.
Row 8 As row 2.
These 8 rows form the patt.

Pattern

Row 1 (RS) P4, *K9, P4, rep from * to end.
Row 2 K4, *P9, K4, rep from * to end.
Row 3 P4, *K3, C6F, P4, rep from * to end.
Row 4 As row 2.
Rows 5 and 6 As rows 1 and 2.
Row 7 P4, *C6B, K3, P4, rep from * to end.
Row 8 As row 2.
These 8 rows form the patt.

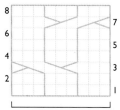

Panel of 9 stitches

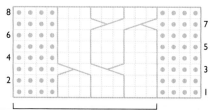

13-stitch repeat

variation

Worked on a multiple
of 16 stitches plus 4.

3.75mm
(Size 5)

DK Alpaca

Single panel

Row 1 (RS) K12.
Row 2 P12.
Row 3 K4, C8F.
Row 4 As row 2.
Rows 5 and 6 As rows 1 and 2.
Row 7 C8B, K4.
Row 8 As row 2.
These 8 rows form the patt.

Pattern

Row 1 (RS) P4, *K12, P4, rep from * to end.
Row 2 K4, *P12, K4, rep from * to end.
Row 3 P4, *K4, C8F, P4, rep from * to end.
Row 4 As row 2.
Rows 5 and 6 As rows 1 and 2.
Row 7 P4, *C8B, K4, P4, rep from * to end.
Row 8 As row 2.
These 8 rows form the patt.

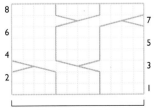

Panel of 12 stitches

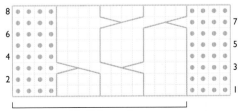

16-stitch repeat

circular cable

Panel of 16 stitches. Worked on a background of reverse stocking stitch.

5mm
(Size 8)

Aran

Pattern

Row 1 (RS) K1, P2, (K2, P2) 3 times, K1.
Row 2 P1, K2, (P2, K2) 3 times, P1.
Row 3 C8B rib, C8F rib.
Row 4 As row 2.
Rows 5 and 6 As rows 1 and 2.
Row 7 K1, P2, K2, P2, MB-2, P2, K2, P2, K1.
Row 8 As row 2.
Rows 9 and 10 As rows 1 and 2.
Row 11 C8F rib, C8B rib.
Row 12 As row 2.
Rows 13 to 16 Work rows 1 and 2 twice.
These 16 rows form the patt.

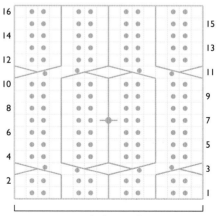

Panel of 16 stitches

variation

Panel of 16 stitches. Worked on a
background of reverse stocking stitch.

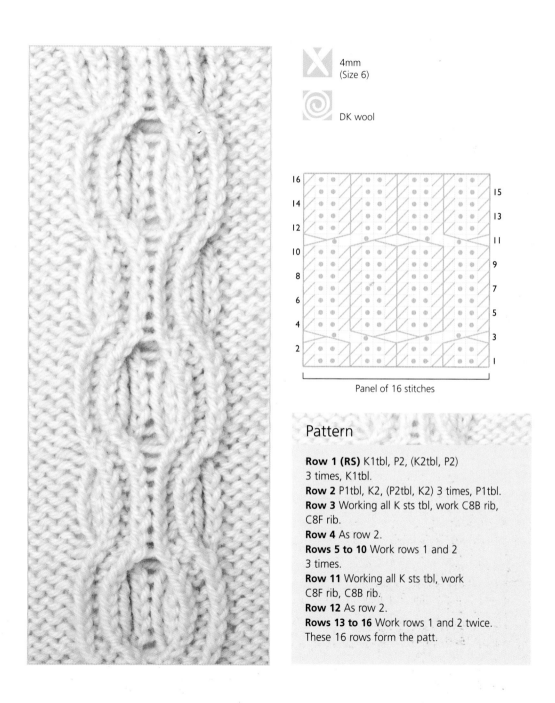

4mm
(Size 6)

DK wool

16   15
14   13
12   11
10   9
8   7
6   5
4   3
2   1

Panel of 16 stitches

Pattern

Row 1 (RS) K1tbl, P2, (K2tbl, P2)
3 times, K1tbl.
Row 2 P1tbl, K2, (P2tbl, K2) 3 times, P1tbl.
Row 3 Working all K sts tbl, work C8B rib,
C8F rib.
Row 4 As row 2.
Rows 5 to 10 Work rows 1 and 2
3 times.
Row 11 Working all K sts tbl, work
C8F rib, C8B rib.
Row 12 As row 2.
Rows 13 to 16 Work rows 1 and 2 twice.
These 16 rows form the patt.

woven cable

Panel of 24 stitches. Worked on a
background of reverse stocking stitch.

 4mm
(Size 6)

DK wool

Pattern

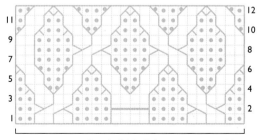

Row 1 (WS) K2, P4, (K4, P4) twice, K2.
Row 2 P2, C4F, P4, W4, P4, C4B, P2.
Row 3 As row 1.
Row 4 P1, Tw3R, Tw3L, (P2, Tw3R, Tw3L) twice, P1.
Row 5 K1, P2, (K2, P2) 5 times, K1.
Row 6 (Tw3R, P2, Tw3L) 3 times.
Row 7 P2, K4, (P4, K4) twice, P2.
Row 8 K2, P4, C4F, P4, C4B, P4, K2.

Row 9 As row 7.
Row 10 (Tw3L, P2, Tw3R) 3 times.
Row 11 As row 5.
Row 12 P1, Tw3L, Tw3R, (P2, Tw3L, Tw3R) twice, P1.
These 12 rows form the patt.

Panel of 24 stitches

variation

Panel of 24 stitches. Worked on a background of reverse stocking stitch.

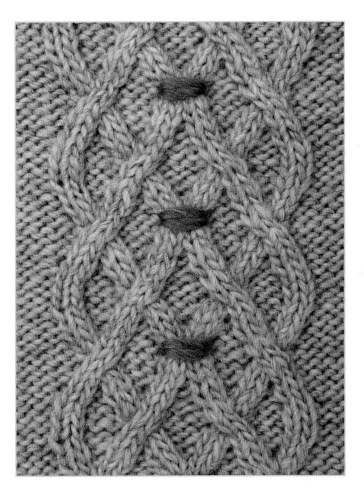

Embellishment

Stitches on row 2 are wrapped using yarn in a contrasting colour. You could add beads to a length of yarn and wrap this for added detail.

 5mm
(Size 8)

DK wool

Pattern

Row 1 (WS) K2, P4, (K4, P4) twice, K2.
Row 2 P2, C4F, P4, using yarn in a contrasting colour W4, then using main colour P4, C4B, P2.
Row 3 As row 1.
Row 4 P1, Tw3R, Tw3L, (P2, Tw3R, Tw3L) twice, P1.
Row 5 K1, P2, (K2, P2) 5 times, K1.
Row 6 (Tw3R, P2, Tw3L) 3 times.

Row 7 P2, K4, (P4, K4) twice, P2.
Row 8 K2, P4, C4F, P4, C4B, P4, K2.
Row 9 As row 7.
Row 10 (Tw3L, P2, Tw3R) 3 times.
Row 11 Rep row 5.
Row 12 P1, Tw3L, Tw3R, (P2, Tw3L, Tw3R) twice, P1.
These 12 rows form the patt.

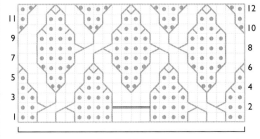

Panel of 24 stitches

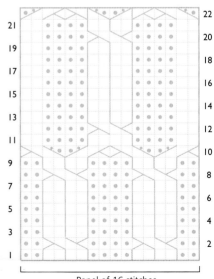

intertwined cable

Panel of 16 stitches. Worked on a
background of reverse stocking stitch.

X 5mm
(Size 8)

Aran

Pattern

Row 1 (WS) K2, P4, K4, P4, K2.
Row 2 P2, C4F, P4, C4F, P2.
Row 3 K2, P4, K4, P4, K2.
Row 4 P2, K4, P4, K4, P2.
Rows 5 and 6 As rows 3 and 4.
Row 7 As row 3.
Rows 8 and 9 As rows 2 and 3.
Row 10 (Tw4R, Tw4L) twice.
Row 11 P2, K4, P4, K4, P2.
Row 12 K2, P4, C4F, P4, K2.

Row 13 P2, K4, P4, K4, P2.
Row 14 K2, P4, K4, P4, K2.
Rows 15 to 19 Work rows 13
and 14 twice, then work row
13 again.
Rows 20 and 21 As rows 12
and 13.
Row 22 (Tw4L, Tw4R) twice.
These 22 rows form the patt.

Panel of 16 stitches

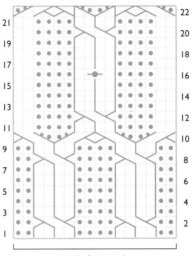

variation

Panel of 16 stitches. Worked on a background of reverse stocking stitch.

Panel of 16 stitches

X 3.75mm (Size 5)

◎ DK Alpaca

Pattern

Row 1 (WS) K2, P4, K4, P4, K2.
Row 2 P2, C4F, P4, C4F, P2.
Row 3 K2, P4, K4, P4, K2.
Row 4 P2, K4, P4, K4, P2.
Rows 5 and 6 As rows 3 and 4.
Row 7 As row 3.
Rows 8 and 9 As rows 2 and 3.
Row 10 (Tw4R, Tw4L) twice.
Row 11 P2, K4, P4, K4, P2.
Row 12 K2, P4, C4F, P4, K2.
Row 13 P2, K4, P4, K4, P2.
Row 14 K2, P4, K4, P4, K2.
Row 15 As row 13.
Row 16 K2, P4, K1, MB-2, K1, P4, K2.
Rows 17 and 18 As rows 13 and 14.
Row 19 As row 13.
Rows 20 and 21 As rows 12 and 13.
Row 22 (Tw4L, Tw4R) twice.
These 22 rows form the patt.

project 5: hot water bottle cover

Snuggle up with a cosy hot water bottle wrapped in a baby-soft alpaca cover. Small mother-of-pearl buttons are used to fasten the back opening.

YOU WILL NEED
- 150g DK yarn in light grey
- 3.75mm (size 5) knitting needles
- 4 buttons
- Hot water bottle

SIZE
To fit a hot water bottle 20.5 x 25cm (8 x 10in)

TENSION
1 patt rep of 9 sts to 3cm and 29 rows to 10cm (4in) over cable patt, with patt slightly opened out

TO FINISH
Block back and front to size. Join side seams, reversing seam for 2.5cm (1in) at top of cuff. Press seams lightly using a warm iron over a damp cloth. Sew a button to the twist of the first and every alternate cable. Using four 4m (4½yd) lengths of yarn, make a twisted cord (see page 134). Starting at centre front, thread the cord under each twisted stitch and over each cable around base of cuff. Insert hot water bottle, fold front over to the back and fasten. Draw up the cord to fit the neck of the bottle and tie in a bow to secure. Knot and trim the ends. Turn back top of cuff for 2.5cm (1in).

Pattern

BACK
Using 3.75mm (size 5) needles cast on 68 sts.
Work in Cable and Braid patt as follows:
Row 1 (RS) P2, K1tbl, P2, *K4, P2, K1tbl, P2, rep from * to end.
Row 2 K2, P1tbl, K2, *P4, K2, P1tbl, K2, rep from * to end.
Row 3 P2, K1tbl, P2, *C4B, P2, K1tbl, P2, rep from * to end.
Row 4 As row 2.
Rows 5 and 6 As rows 1 and 2.
These 6 rows form the patt.
Cont in patt until work measures 20.5cm (8in) from beg, ending row 6.
Shape top
Cont in patt, cast off 5 sts at beg of next 6 rows and 4 sts at beg of foll 2 rows. 30 sts.
Patt 1 row.
Next row Patt 3, *puk, patt 3, pup, patt 3, puk, patt 3, rep from * to end. 39 sts.
Now work cuff in twisted rib as follows:
Next row (RS) P1, *K1tbl, P1, rep from * to end.
Next row K1, *P1tbl, K1, rep from * to end.
Rep these 2 rows for 9cm (3½in), ending with a WS row. Cast off in patt.

FRONT
Using 3.75mm (size 5) needles cast on 61 sts.
Work in twisted rib as follows:
Next row (RS) K1tbl, *P1, K1tbl, rep from * to end.
Next row P1tbl, *K1, P1tbl, rep from * to end.
Rep these 2 rows once more.
Buttonhole row Rib 6, yrn, P2 tog, *rib 14, yrn, P2 tog, rep from * to last 5 sts, rib to end.
Work 5 more rows in twisted rib, so ending with a WS row.
Next row P2, K1tbl, P2, *K2, puk, K1, P2, K1tbl, P2, rep from * to end. 68 sts.
Beg row 2, work in patt as given for back until work measures 28cm (11in) from beg, ending row 6.
Shape top and work cuff as given for back.

project 6: hand muff

The gorgeous fabric used for this sophisticated hand muff is created by knitting a strand of DK yarn and fine mohair together.

designer's tip

The length of the strap can be adjusted to ensure the muff sits in the correct position, making it comfortable to wear. Simply ease the bead through the strap at the required position to fasten.

YOU WILL NEED

- 100g DK yarn in cream (A)
- 75g fine mohair yarn in fawn (B)
- 5mm (size 8) and 6.5mm (size 10½) knitting needles
- 1 long wooden bead

SIZE

33cm (13in) long and 20.5cm (8in) diameter

TENSION

1 patt rep of 14 sts to 6.5cm (2½in) and 21 rows to 10cm (4in) over cable patt on size 6.5mm (10½) needles, using one strand of A and B together

TO FINISH

Block knitting to size. Fold muff in half lengthways and join the seam. Press seam lightly with a warm iron over a damp cloth.

DETACHABLE STRAP

Using four 5m (5½yd) lengths in each of A and B together, make a twisted cord (see page 134), tying a knot with the loose ends only about 10cm (4in) from the end. Use the ends to secure the long bead close to the knot. Thread the strap through the muff and fasten (see designer's tip).

Pattern

TO MAKE (made in one piece)

Using 5mm (size 8) needles and one strand each of A and B together throughout, cast on 74 sts.
Work in rib as follows:
Next row K2, *P2, K2, rep from * to end.
Next row P2, *K2, P2, rep from * to end.
Rep these 2 rows once more, then work the first of these 2 rows again.
Next row Rib 6, K into front and back of next 2 sts, *rib 10, K into front and back of next 2 sts, rep from * to last 6 sts, rib to end. 86 sts.
Change to 6.5mm (size 10½) needles.
Cont in Simple 8-stitch Cable patt as follows:
Row 1 (RS) P4, K8, *P6, K8, rep from * to last 4 sts, P4.
Row 2 K4, P8, *K6, P8, rep from * to last 4 sts, K4.
Rows 3 and 4 As rows 1 and 2.
Row 5 P4, C8F, *P6, C8F, rep from * to last 4 sts, P4.
Row 6 As row 2.
Rows 7 to 10 Work rows 1 and 2 twice.
These 10 rows form the patt.
Cont in patt until work measures 30cm (12in) from beg, ending row 8.
Change to 5mm (size 8) needles.
Next row K2, P2, K2, (P2 tog) twice, *K2, (P2, K2) twice, (P2 tog) twice, rep from * to last 6 sts, K2, P2, K2. 74 sts.
Rib 5 rows. Cast off.

project 7: cushion and bolster

Sit back and relax on these stunning cushions.
Worked in one piece, the cushion and bolster
are the perfect additions for your sofa.

Cushion and bolster pattern

CUSHION (made in one piece)
Using 7mm (size 10½) needles cast on
82 sts.
Work in Travelling Cable patt as follows:
Row 1 (RS) P3, K6, *P4, K6, rep from *
to last 3 sts, P3.
Row 2 K3, P6, *K4, P6, rep from *
to last 3 sts, K3.
Rows 3 and 4 As rows 1 and 2.
Row 5 P3, C6F, *P4, C6F, rep from *
to last 3 sts, P3.
Row 6 As row 2.
Rows 7 to 12 Work rows 1 and 2
three times.
Row 13 P3, C6B, *P4, C6B, rep from *
to last 3 sts, P3.
Row 14 As row 2.
Rows 15 and 16 As rows 1 and 2.
These 16 rows form the patt.

Cont in patt until work measures
99cm (39in) from beg, ending with
a WS row.
Now work the ribbed band.
Next row K1, (P2, K2) twice, *P4, K2,
P2, K2, rep from * to last 3 sts, P2, K1.
Next row P1, (K2, P2) twice, *K4, P2,
K2, P2, rep from * to last 3 sts, K2, P1.
Rep these 2 rows once more, then work
the first of these 2 rows again.
Cast off knitwise.

BOLSTER (made in one piece)
Work as given for cushion until work
measures 53cm (21in) from beg, ending
with a RS row. Cast off knitwise.

YOU WILL NEED
For cushion:
• 500g bulky yarn in lavender
• 7mm (size 10½) knitting needles
• 4 large buttons
• Square cushion pad
For bolster:
• 200g bulky yarn in lavender
• 7mm (size 10½) knitting needles
• Bolster pad
• 1m (1yd) leather or cotton cord

SIZE
Cushion, 49cm (19½in) square
Bolster, 49cm (19½in) circumference
and 53cm (21in) long

TENSION
1 patt rep of 10 sts to 6.5cm (2½in)
and 19 rows to 10cm (4in) over cable
patt, with patt slightly opened out

TO FINISH CUSHION
Block knitting to size. Lay the knitting, with RS facing,
on a flat surface and fold the top down, then fold
the bottom up, overlapping the ribbed band onto
the bottom section. Pin the side edges. Join the side
seams, working through all three layers at the overlap.
Press seams lightly using a warm iron over a damp
cloth. Turn the cover to the right side and insert the
cushion pad. Working through the double thickness,
sew and tie a button (see page 137) to the first and
every alternate reverse stocking section between
cables to close the cover.

TO FINISH BOLSTER
Block knitting to size. Fold the knitting in half
lengthways and join the seam. Press seam lightly using
a warm iron over a damp cloth. Using yarn double,
leaving a long end, work a row of running stitch
along the cast-on edge. Do not fasten off, but pull
the ends up to gather the knitting. Tie a knot close to
the knitting to secure, then sew in the ends. Turn the
cover to the right side. Insert the bolster pad. Wrap
the length of cord several times around the opening
close to the pad and tie a bow to secure. Trim ends to
length required.

project 8: throw and cushion

This textured throw will look stunning draped over a chair or the end of a bed. To complete the setting add a matching cushion.

Throw pattern

TO MAKE (made in strips)
Using 5mm (size 8) needles and A, cast on 104 sts for one strip.
Work in Elongated Cable patt as follows:
Row 1 (RS) P4, *K6, P4, rep from * to end.
Row 2 K4, *P6, K4, rep from * to end.
Row 3 P4, *C6F, P4, rep from * to end.
Row 4 As row 2.
Rows 5 to 8 Work rows 1 and 2 twice.
Row 9 As row 3.
Row 10 As row 2.
Rows 11 to 18 Work rows 1 and 2 four times.
These 18 rows form the patt.
Rep them 3 times more.
Cut off A. Join on B and work the 18 patt rows 4 times.
Cut off B. Join on C and work the 18 patt rows 4 times.
Cut off C. Join on D and work the 18 patt rows 4 times, then work rows 1 to 9 again.
Cast off knitwise.
Make another strip in the same way.

YOU WILL NEED
For throw:
• 100g DK yarn in each of natural (A), brown (B), grey (C) and dark brown (D) for each strip
• 5mm (Size 8) knitting needles
• Crochet hook or hairpin for fringing
For cushion:
• 150g DK yarn in brown (B)
• Pair of 5mm (size 8) knitting needles
• 5 buttons
• Square cushion pad

SIZE
Throw: each strip measures 40 x 119cm (15½ x 47in), excluding fringe
Cushion: 34 x 35cm (13¼ x 13¾in)

TENSION
1 patt rep of 10 sts to 4cm (1½in) and 25 rows to 10cm (4in) over cable patt, with patt slightly opened out
19 sts and 26 rows to 10cm (4in) over st st

TO FINISH THROW

Block strips to size. Sew in the ends. Join the strips along one long edge, having the seam on the right side. Press seam lightly using a warm iron over a damp cloth. Using five 24cm (9½in) lengths of yarn together, knot a fringe (see page 135) evenly along each short edge (see designer's tip on page 90). Trim the ends.

Cushion pattern

TO MAKE (made in one piece)
Using 5mm (size 8) needles and B, cast on
66 sts.
Work the ribbed band as follows:
Rib row 1 (RS) K2, *P2, K2, rep from *
to end.
Rib row 2 P2, *K2, P2, rep from * to end.
Rep these 2 rows 3 times more, then work
row 1 again.
Next row Rib 28, P into front and back of
next 2 sts, rib 6, P into front and back of next
2 sts, rib to end. 70 sts.
Now work in st st with Elongated Cable panel
as follows:
Row 1 (RS) K23, P4, (K6, P4) twice, K to end.
Row 2 P23, K4, (P6, K4) twice, P to end.
Row 3 K23, P4, (C6F, P4) twice, K to end.
Row 4 As row 2.
Rows 5 to 8 Work rows 1 and 2 twice.
Row 9 As row 3.
Row 10 As row 2.
Rows 11 to 18 Work rows 1 and 2 four times.
These 18 rows form the patt.
Cont in patt until work measures 66cm (26in)
from beg, ending with a RS row.
Next row Patt 28, (P2 tog) twice, patt 6,
(P2 tog) twice, patt to end. 66 sts.
Now work the 2 rib rows 5 times.
Cast off.

TO FINISH CUSHION

Block knitting to size. Fold knitting in half widthways
and pin side seams. Join the seams. Press seams
lightly using a warm iron over a damp cloth. Insert
the cushion pad. Mark five button positions along
the ribbed band, the first and last 5cm (2in) from
side seams and the others evenly spaced between.
Sew on the buttons, sewing through both ribbed
bands to close the cover.

designer's tip

The throw featured has been made with
two strips. You can adjust the width by adding
as many strips as required. Simply knit each
strip, then join the strips together, with the
seam on the right side, and finish the short
ends with fringing.
The fringing at the cast-on edge has been
worked using two strands of A and B and one
strand of C. The fringing at the cast-off edge has
been worked using two strands of B and D and
one strand of C.
The quantities listed are for making one strip
with fringing.

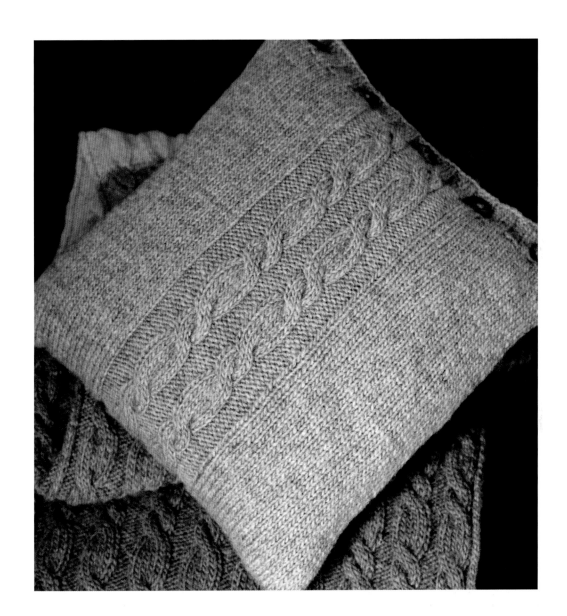

lesson 12

cable patterns

All-over cable patterns are created simply by working the cable design right across a piece of knitting. The given number – or multiple – of stitches that forms the cable is repeated without a break to form a continuous rhythmic texture. Patterns may be worked in vertical, horizontal or diagonal lines, and even in squares. The result is an impressive and richly textured fabric that can be used in many ways.

Worked with fine yarn, all-over cable patterns can create delicate and pretty garments and accessories. Alternatively, exploit the bold combination of modern bulky yarns and large needles to create rugged all-weather sweaters, eye-catching cushion covers or deliciously cosy textured throws.

In this book the multiple of stitches that creates the all-over pattern is indicated above each knitted swatch, together with the number of stitches that should be worked at each end to balance the pattern.

For example, the pattern shown here is formed with a multiple of 12 stitches plus an extra 14 stitches.

You will need to cast on a multiple of 12 stitches – 24, 36 or 48, for example – depending on the width of fabric you want to create, plus 14 more stitches. These extra stitches at the beginning or end of the row are used to balance the pattern and are worked only once on each row.

In the written instructions the multiple to be repeated is shown in brackets, or following an asterisk (*). These stitches are repeated across the row. Some patterns require one or two foundation rows to 'set' the pattern. These rows are shown at the beginning of the pattern, should be worked only once and do not form part of the repeat thereafter.

Pattern

Row 1 (RS) P4, Tw3R, Tw3L, *P6, Tw3R, Tw3L, rep from * to last 4 sts, P4.
Row 2 K4, P2, K2, P2, *K6, P2, K2, P2, rep from * to last 4 sts, K4.
Row 3 P3, Tw3R, P2, Tw3L, *P4, Tw3R, P2, Tw3L, rep from * to last 3 sts, P3.
Row 4 K3, P2, *K4, P2, rep from * to last 3 sts, K3.
Row 5 *P2, Tw3R, P4, Tw3L, rep from * to last 2 sts, P2.
Row 6 K2, P2, K6, *P2, K2, P2, K6, rep from * to last 4 sts, P2, K2.
Row 7 P1, *Tw3R, P6, Tw3L, rep from * to last st, P1.
Row 8 K1, P2, K8, *P4, K8, rep from * to last 3 sts, P2, K1.
Row 9 P1, K2, P8, *C4B, P8, rep from * to last 3 sts, K2, P1.

Row 10 As row 8.
Row 11 P1, *Tw3L, P6, Tw3R, rep from * to last st, P1.
Row 12 As row 6.
Row 13 *P2, Tw3L, P4, Tw3R, rep from * to last 2 sts, P2.
Row 14 As row 4.
Row 15 P3, Tw3L, P2, Tw3R, *P4, Tw3L, P2, Tw3R, rep from * to last 3 sts, P3.
Row 16 As row 2.
Row 17 P4, Tw3L, Tw3R, *P6, Tw3L, Tw3R, rep from * to last 4 sts, P4.
Row 18 K5, P4, *K8, P4, rep from * to last 5 sts, K5.
Row 19 P5, C4B, *P8, C4B, rep from * to last 5 sts, P5.
Row 20 As row 18.
These 20 rows form the patt.

simple diamonds

This sample shows two pattern repeats.
Worked on a multiple of 12 stitches plus 14.

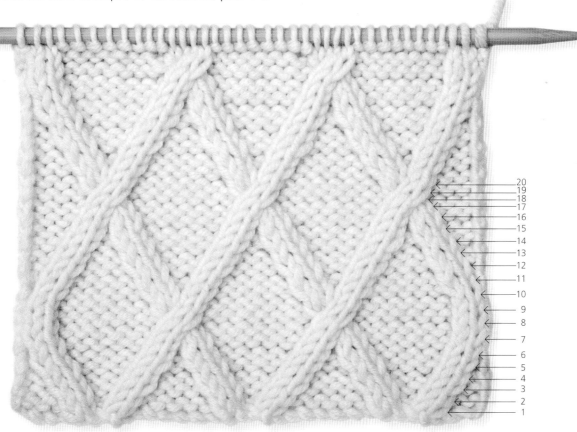

20
19
18
17
16
15
14
13
12
11
10
9
8
7
6
5
4
3
2
1

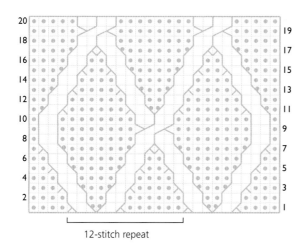

12-stitch repeat

Practice pattern

Use this pattern to work through
the step-by-step exercise overleaf
to make the sample as shown.

 5mm
(Size 8)

 Aran

twisting stitches

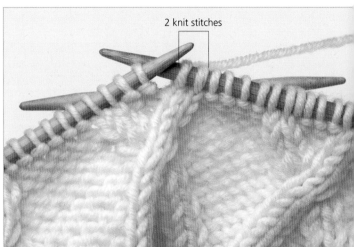

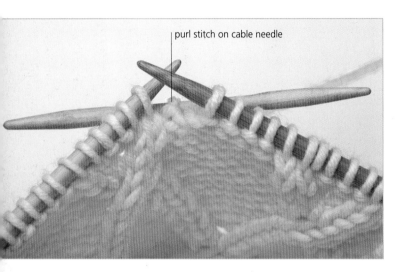

purl stitch on cable needle

2 knit stitches

1 For a diagonal line of stitches sloping to the right, a purl stitch and two knit stitches change places (abbreviated as Tw3R). On a right-side row, work to within one stitch of the knit stitches. Slip the next stitch (a purl stitch) onto a cable needle and leave at the back of the work.

2 Knit the next two stitches from the left-hand needle – the first two stitches of the diamond. The stitch on the cable needle remains at the back of the work.

3 Now purl the stitch from the cable needle. The two knit stitches have moved one stitch to the right and now precede the purl stitch.

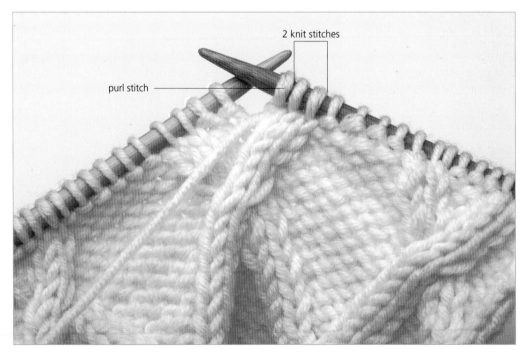

2 knit stitches

purl stitch

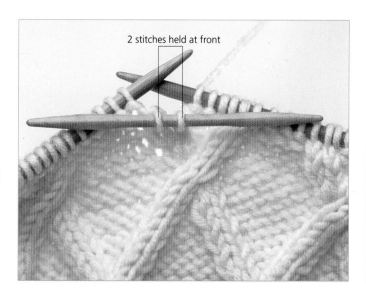

2 stitches held at front

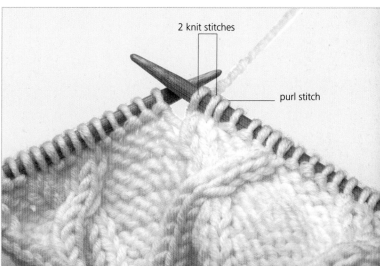

2 knit stitches

purl stitch

4 For a diagonal line of stitches sloping to the left, two knit stitches and a purl stitch change places (abbreviated as Tw3L). On a right-side row, work to within the two knit stitches. Slip the next two stitches onto a cable needle and leave at the front of the work.

5 Purl the next stitch from the left-hand needle, then knit the two stitches from the cable needle. If you have difficulty knitting the stitches from the cable needle, slip them back onto the left-hand needle and knit them in the usual way.

6 By slanting stitches to the right and left on every alternate row the number of purl stitches between the twists will increase, while the number of purl stitches outside the twists will decrease. Twisting stitches in this way forms a diamond pattern.

cable and ridge

This sample shows two pattern repeats. Worked on a multiple of 13 stitches plus 9.

5mm
(Size 8)

Aran

Pattern

Row 1 (RS) P9, *K4, P9, rep from * to end.
Row 2 K1, (P3, K1) twice, *P4, K1, (P3, K1) twice, rep from * to end.
Row 3 P1, (K3, P1) twice, *C4B, P1, (K3, P1) twice, rep from * to end.
Row 4 As row 2.
These 4 rows form the patt.

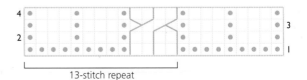

13-stitch repeat

variation

Worked on a multiple
of 19 stitches plus 13.

5mm
(Size 8)

DK wool

Pattern

Row 1 (RS) P13, *K6, P13, rep from * to end.
Row 2 K1, (P5, K1) twice, *P6, K1, (P5, K1) twice, rep from * to end.
Row 3 P1, (K5, P1) twice, *C6B, P1, (K5, P1) twice, rep from * to end.
Row 4 As row 2.
Row 5 P1, (K5, P1) twice, *K6, P1, (K5, P1) twice, rep from * to end.
Row 6 As row 2.
These 6 rows form the patt.

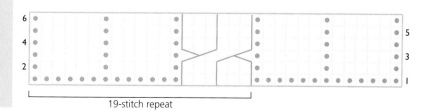

19-stitch repeat

cable knot check

This sample shows two pattern repeats. Worked on a multiple of 12 stitches plus 12.

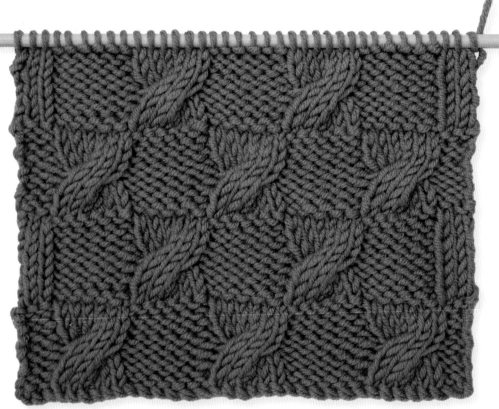

5.5mm (Size 9)

Aran

Pattern

Row 1 (RS) P3, K6, *P6, K6, rep from * to last 3 sts, P3.

Row 2 K3, P6, *K6, P6, rep from * to last 3 sts, K3.

Rows 3 and 4 As rows 1 and 2.

Row 5 P3, C6B, *P6, C6B, rep from * to last 3 sts, P3.

Row 6 As row 2.

Rows 7 and 8 As rows 1 and 2.

Row 9 K3, P6, *K6, P6, rep from * to last 3 sts, K3.

Row 10 P3, K6, *P6, K6, rep from * to last 3 sts, P3.

Rows 11 and 12 As rows 9 and 10.

Row 13 K3, P6, *C6B, P6, rep from * to last 3 sts, K3.

Row 14 As row 10.

Rows 15 and 16 As rows 9 and 10. These 16 rows form the patt.

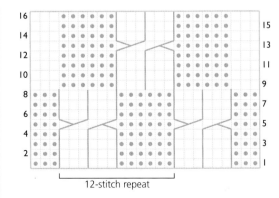

12-stitch repeat

variation

Worked on a multiple
of 12 stitches plus 12.

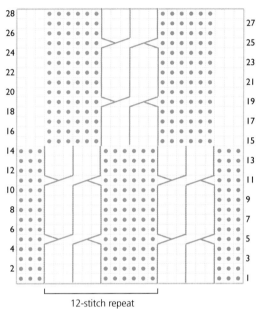

12-stitch repeat

Pattern

 4mm
(Size 6)

 DK cotton

Row 1 (RS) P3, K6, *P6, K6, rep from * to last 3 sts, P3.
Row 2 K3, P6, *K6, P6, rep from * to last 3 sts, K3.
Rows 3 and 4 As rows 1 and 2.
Row 5 P3, C6B, *P6, C6B, rep from * to last 3 sts, P3.
Row 6 As row 2.
Rows 7 to 10 Work rows 1 and 2 twice.
Row 11 As row 5.
Row 12 As row 2.
Rows 13 and 14 As rows 1 and 2.
Row 15 K3, P6, *K6, P6, rep from * to last 3 sts, K3.

Row 16 P3, K6, *P6, K6, rep from * to last 3 sts, P3.
Rows 17 and 18 As rows 15 and 16.
Row 19 K3, P6, *C6B, P6, rep from * to last 3 sts, K3.
Row 20 As row 16.
Rows 21 to 24 Work rows 15 and 16 twice.
Row 25 As row 19.
Row 26 As row 16.
Rows 27 and 28 As rows 15 and 16.
These 28 rows form the patt.

wavy cable check

This sample shows two pattern repeats. Worked on a multiple of 14 stitches plus 8.

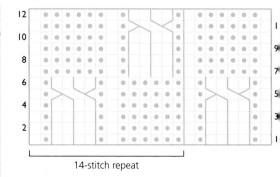

X 5mm (Size 8)

◎ Aran

Pattern

Row 1 (RS) K1, P1, K4, P1, K1, *P6, K1, P1, K4, P1, K1, rep from * to end.
Row 2 P1, K1, P4, K1, P1, *K6, P1, K1, P4, K1, P1, rep from * to end.
Rows 3 and 4 As rows 1 and 2.
Row 5 K1, P1, C4F, P1, K1, *P6, K1, P1, C4F, P1, K1, rep from * to end.
Row 6 As row 2.
Row 7 K1, P6, K1, *P1, K4, P1, K1, P6, K1, rep from * to end.

Row 8 P1, K6, P1, *K1, P4, K1, P1, K6, P1, rep from * to end.
Rows 9 and 10 As rows 7 and 8.
Row 11 K1, P6, K1, *P1, C4F, P1, K1, P6, K1, rep from * to end.
Row 12 As row 8.
These 12 rows form the patt.

variation

Worked on a multiple
of 18 stitches plus 10.

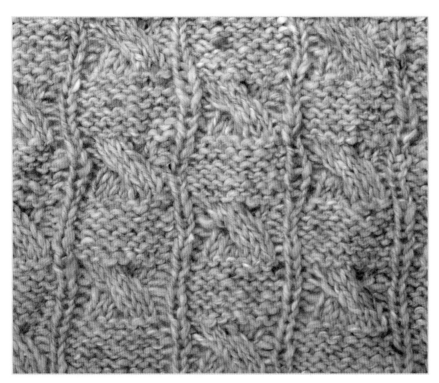

5mm
(Size 8)

Aran tweed

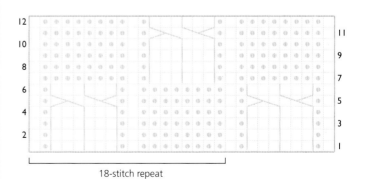

Pattern

Row 1 (RS) K1, P1, K6, P1, K1, *P8, K1, P1, K6, P1, K1, rep from * to end.
Row 2 P1, K1, P6, K1, P1, *K8, P1, K1, P6, K1, P1, rep from * to end.
Rows 3 and 4 As rows 1 and 2.
Row 5 K1, P1, C6F, P1, K1, *P8, K1, P1, C6F, P1, K1, rep from * to end.
Row 6 As row 2.

Row 7 K1, P8, K1, *P1, K6, P1, K1, P8, K1, rep from * to end.
Row 8 P1, K8, P1, *K1, P6, K1, P1, K8, P1, rep from * to end.
Rows 9 and 10 As rows 7 and 8.
Row 11 K1, P8, K1, *P1, C6F, P1, K1, P8, K1, rep from * to end.
Row 12 As row 8.
These 12 rows form the patt.

18-stitch repeat

cable knot rib

This sample shows two pattern repeats. Worked on a multiple of 14 stitches plus 8.

 4.5mm
(Size 7)

 DK cotton

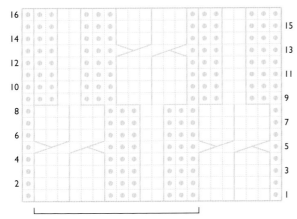

14-stitch repeat

Pattern

Row 1 (RS) P1, K6, *P3, K2, P3, K6, rep from *
to last st, P1.
Row 2 K1, P6, *K3, P2, K3, P6, rep from *
to last st, K1.
Rows 3 and 4 Rep rows 1 and 2.
Row 5 P1, C6B, *P3, K2, P3, C6B, rep from *
to last st, P1.
Row 6 As row 2.
Rows 7 and 8 As rows 1 and 2.
Row 9 P3, K2, P3, *K6, P3, K2, P3, rep from *
to end.

Row 10 K3, P2, K3, *P6, K3, P2, K3, rep
from * to end.
Rows 11 and 12 As rows 9 and 10.
Row 13 P3, K2, P3, *C6B, P3, K2, P3, rep
from * to end.
Row 14 As row 10.
Rows 15 and 16 As rows 9 and 10.
These 16 rows form the patt.

horseshoe trellis

This sample shows one pattern repeat. Worked on a multiple of 16 stitches plus 18.

5mm
(Size 8)

Aran tweed

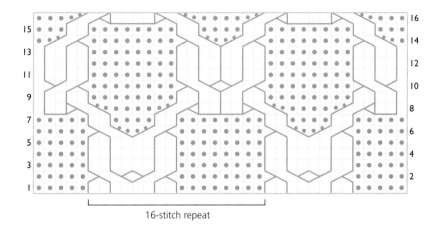

16-stitch repeat

Pattern

Row 1 (WS) K5, P8, *K8, P8, rep from * to last 5 sts, K5.

Row 2 P5, C4B, C4F, *P8, C4B, C4F, rep from * to last 5 sts, P5.

Row 3 As row 1.

Row 4 P5, K8, *P8, K8, rep from * to last 5 sts, P5.

Row 5 As row 1.

Row 6 P5, Tw4R, Tw4L, *P8, Tw4R, Tw4L, rep from * to last 5 sts, P5.

Row 7 K5, P2, K4, P2, *K8, P2, K4, P2, rep from * to last 5 sts, K5.

Row 8 K3, Tw4R, P4, Tw4L, *K4, Tw4R, P4, Tw4L, rep from * to last 3 sts, K3.

Row 9 P5, K8, *P8, K8, rep from * to last 5 sts, P5.

Row 10 K1, *C4F, P8, C4B, rep from * to last st, K1.

Row 11 As row 9.

Row 12 K5, P8, *K8, P8, rep from * to last 5 sts, K5.

Row 13 As row 9.

Row 14 P1, *Tw4L, P8, Tw4R, rep from * to last st, P1.

Row 15 K3, P2, K8, *P2, K4, P2, K8, rep from * to last 5 sts, P2, K3.

Row 16 P3, Tw4L, K4, Tw4R, *P4, Tw4L, K4, Tw4R, rep from * to last 3 sts, P3.

These 16 rows form the patt.

lattice and bobbles

This sample shows two pattern repeats. Worked on a multiple of 16 stitches plus 18.

 4mm
(Size 6)

 DK

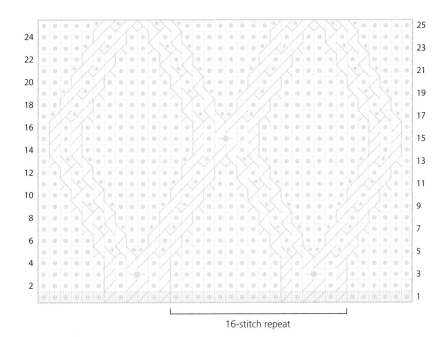

16-stitch repeat

Pattern

Row 1 (RS) P6, *K1tbl, P1, K2tbl, P1, K1tbl, P10, rep from * to end, finishing last rep P6.
Row 2 K6, *P1tbl, K1, P2tbl, K1, P1tbl, K10, rep from * to end, finishing last rep K6.
Row 3 P6, *K1tbl, P1, MB-2, P1, K1tbl, P10, rep from * to end, finishing last rep P6.
Row 4 As row 2.
Row 5 P5, *(Tw2R) twice, (Tw2L) twice, P8, rep from * to end, finishing last rep P5.
Row 6 and following wrong-side rows K all K sts and P tbl all P sts.
Row 7 P4, *(Tw2R) twice, P2, (Tw2L) twice, P6, rep from * to end, finishing last rep P4.
Row 9 P3, *(Tw2R) twice, P4, (Tw2L) twice, P4, rep from * to end, finishing last rep P3.
Row 11 P2, *(Tw2R) twice, P6, (Tw2L) twice, P2, rep from * to end.

Row 13 P1, *(Tw2R) twice, P8, (Tw2L) twice, rep from * to last st, P1.
Row 15 (P1, K1tbl) twice, P10, *K1tbl, P1, MB-2, P1, K1tbl, P10, rep from * to last 4 sts, (K1tbl, P1) twice.
Row 17 P1, *(Tw2L) twice, P8, (Tw2R) twice, rep from * to last st, P1.
Row 19 P2, *(Tw2L) twice, P6, (Tw2R) twice, P2, rep from * to end.
Row 21 P3, *(Tw2L) twice, P4, (Tw2R) twice, P4, rep from * to end, finishing last rep P3.
Row 23 P4, *(Tw2L) twice, P2, (Tw2R) twice, P6, rep from * to end, finishing last rep P4.
Row 25 P5, *(Tw2L) twice, (Tw2R) twice, P8, rep from * to end, finishing last rep P5.
Rows 2 to 25 form the patt.

diamonds and bobbles

This sample shows two pattern repeats. Worked on a multiple of 12 stitches plus 14.

5mm
(Size 8)

Aran

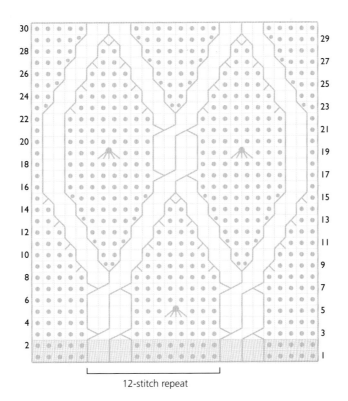

30 · 29
28 · 27
26 · 25
24 · 23
22 · 21
20 · 19
18 · 17
16 · 15
14 · 13
12 · 11
10 · 9
8 · 7
6 · 5
4 · 3
2 · 1

12-stitch repeat

Pattern

Row 1 (RS) P5, K4, *P8, K4, rep from * to last 5 sts, P5.

Row 2 K5, P4, *K8, P4, rep from * to last 5 sts, K5.

Row 3 P5, C4B, *P8, C4B, rep from * to last 5 sts, P5.

Row 4 K5, P4, *K8, P4, rep from * to last 5 sts, K5.

Row 5 P5, K4, *P3, MB-3 over next 2 sts, P3, K4, rep from * to last 5 sts, P5.

Row 6 As row 4.

Rows 7 and 8 As rows 3 and 4.

Row 9 P4, Tw3R, Tw3L, *P6, Tw3R, Tw3L, rep from * to last 4 sts, P4.

Row 10 K4, P2, K2, P2, *K6, P2, K2, P2, rep from * to last 4 sts, K4.

Row 11 P3, Tw3R, P2, Tw3L, *P4, Tw3R, P2, Tw3L, rep from * to last 3 sts, P3.

Row 12 K3, P2, *K4, P2, rep from * to last 3 sts, K3.

Row 13 P2, *Tw3R, P4, Tw3L, P2, rep from * to end.

Row 14 K2, *P2, K6, P2, K2, rep from * to end.

Row 15 P1, *Tw3R, P6, Tw3L, rep from * to last st, P1.

Row 16 K1, P2, K8, *P4, K8, rep from * to last 3 sts, P2, K1.

Row 17 P1, K2, P8, *C4B, P8, rep from * to last 3 sts, K2, P1.

Row 18 K1, P2, K8, *P4, K8, rep from * to last 3 sts, P2, K1.

Row 19 P1, K2, P3, MB-3 over next 2 sts, P3, *K4, P3, MB-3 over next 2 sts, P3, rep from * to last 3 sts, K2, P1.

Rows 20 to 22 Rep rows 16 to 18.

Row 23 P1, *Tw3L, P6, Tw3R, rep from * to last st, P1.

Row 24 K2, *P2, K6, P2, K2, rep from * to end.

Row 25 P2, *Tw3L, P4, Tw3R, P2, rep from * to end.

Row 26 K3, P2, *K4, P2, rep from * to last 3 sts, K3.

Row 27 P3, Tw3L, P2, Tw3R, *P4, Tw3L, P2, Tw3R, rep from * to last 3 sts, P3.

Row 28 K4, P2, K2, P2, *K6, P2, K2, P2, rep from * to last 4 sts, K4.

Row 29 P4, Tw3L, Tw3R, *P6, Tw3L, Tw3R, rep from * to last 4 sts, P4.

Row 30 K5, P4, *K8, P4, rep from * to last 5 sts, K5.

Rows 3 to 30 form the patt.

staggered cables

This sample shows two pattern repeats. Worked on a multiple of 14 stitches plus 8.

5mm (Size 8)

DK wool

Pattern

Row 1 (RS) *P1, K6, rep from * to last st, P1.

Row 2 *K1, P6, rep from * to last st, K1.

Row 3 P1, K6, *P1, C6B, P1, K6, rep from * to last st, P1.

Row 4 As row 2.

Rows 5 to 8 Work rows 1 and 2 twice.

Row 9 As row 3.

Row 10 As row 2.

Rows 11 and 12 Rep rows 1 and 2.

Row 13 P1, C6B, *P1, K6, P1, C6B, rep from * to last st, P1.

Row 14 As row 2.

Rows 15 to 18 Work rows 1 and 2 twice.

Row 19 As row 13.

Row 20 As row 2.
These 20 rows form the patt.

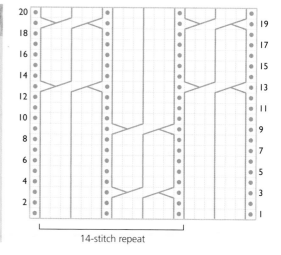

14-stitch repeat

variation

Worked on a multiple
of 10 stitches plus 6.

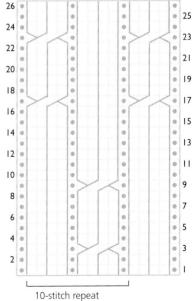

4.5mm
(Size 7)

DK cotton

Pattern

Row 1 (RS) *P1, K4, rep from * to last st, P1.

Row 2 *K1, P4, rep from * to last st, K1.

Row 3 P1, K4, *P1, C4B, P1, K4, rep from * to last st, P1.

Row 4 As row 2.

Rows 5 to 8 Work rows 1 and 2 twice.

Row 9 As row 3.

Row 10 As row 2.

Rows 11 to 16 Work rows 1 and 2 three times.

Row 17 P1, C4B, *P1, K4, P1, C4B, rep from * to last st, P1.

Row 18 As row 2.

Rows 19 to 22 Work rows 1 and 2 twice.

Row 23 As row 17.

Row 24 As row 2.

Rows 25 and 26 As rows 1 and 2. These 26 rows form the patt.

10-stitch repeat

cable grid

This sample shows three pattern repeats. Worked on a multiple of 12 stitches plus 8.

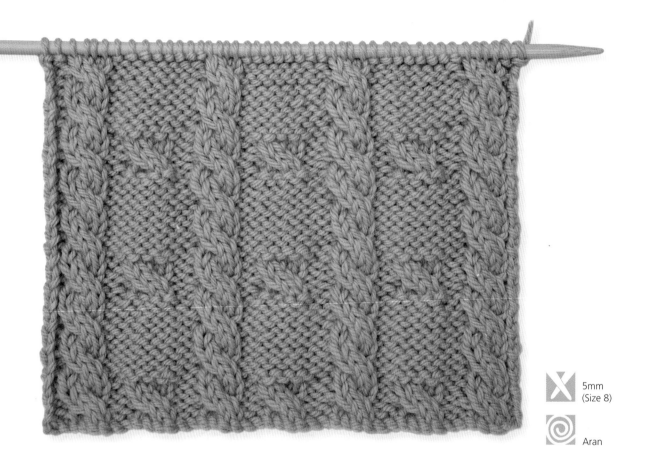

X 5mm
(Size 8)

◎ Aran

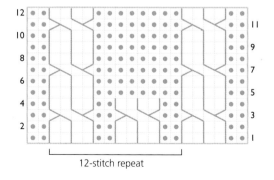

Pattern

Row 1 (RS) P2, *K4, P2, rep from * to end.

Row 2 K2, *P4, K2, rep from * to end.

Row 3 P2, *C4F, P2, rep from * to end.

Row 4 As row 2.

Row 5 P2, K4, *P8, K4, rep from * to last 2 sts, P2.

Row 6 K2, P4, *K8, P4, rep from * to last 2 sts, K2.

Row 7 P2, C4F, *P8, C4F, rep from * to last 2 sts, P2.

Row 8 As row 6.

Rows 9 to 11 Rep rows 5 to 7.

Row 12 As row 6.

These 12 rows form the patt.

12-stitch repeat

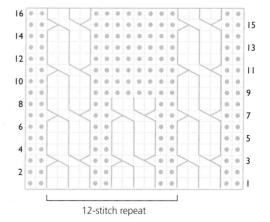

variation

Worked on a multiple
of 12 stitches plus 8.

5mm
(Size 8)

Aran

Pattern

Row 1 (RS) P2, *K4, P2, rep from *
to end.
Row 2 K2, *P4, K2, rep from * to end.
Row 3 P2, *C4F, P2, rep from * to end.
Row 4 As row 2.
Rows 5 and 6 Rep rows 1 and 2.
Row 7 As row 3.
Row 8 As row 2.
Row 9 P2, K4, *P8, K4, rep from * to
last 2 sts, P2.

Row 10 K2, P4, *K8, P4, rep from *
to last 2 sts, K2.
Row 11 P2, C4F, *P8, C4F, rep from *
to last 2 sts, P2.
Row 12 As row 10.
Rows 13 and 14 Rep rows 9 and 10.
Row 15 As row 11.
Row 16 As row 10.
These 16 rows form the patt.

16
14
12
10
8
6
4
2

15
13
11
9
7
5
3
1

12-stitch repeat

interlocking cables

This sample shows two pattern repeats. Worked on a multiple of 16 stitches plus 16.

 3.75mm
(Size 5)

 DK cotton

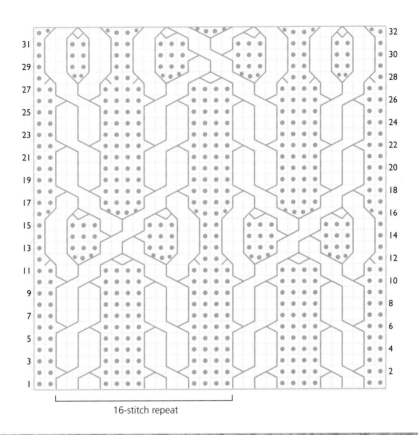

16-stitch repeat

Pattern

Row 1 (WS) K2, P4, *K4, P4, rep from * to last 2 sts, K2.
Row 2 P2, C4F, P4, C4B, *P4, C4F, P4, C4B, rep from * to last 2 sts, P2.
Row 3 As row 1.
Row 4 P2, K4, *P4, K4, rep from * to last 2 sts, P2.
Rows 5 and 6 As rows 1 and 2.
Row 7 As row 1.
Row 8 As row 4.
Rows 9 and 10 As rows 1 and 2.
Row 11 As row 1.
Row 12 P1, *Tw3R, Tw4L, Tw4R, Tw3L, P2, rep from *to end, finishing last rep P1.
Row 13 K1, *P2, K3, P4, K3, P2, K2, rep from * to end, finishing last rep K1.

Row 14 P1, *K2, P3, C4B, P3, K2, P2, rep from * to end, finishing last rep P1.
Row 15 As row 13.
Row 16 P1, *Tw3L, Tw4R, Tw4L, Tw3R, P2, rep from * to end, finishing last rep P1.
Row 17 As row 1.
Row 18 P2, *C4B, P4, C4F, P4, rep from * to end, finishing last rep P2.
Row 19 As row 1.
Row 20 As row 4.
Row 21 As row 1.
Row 22 As row 18.
Row 23 As row 1.
Row 24 As row 4.
Row 25 As row 1.
Row 26 As row 18.

Row 27 As row 1.
Row 28 P1, Tw3R, Tw3L, P2, *Tw3R, Tw4L, Tw4R, Tw3L, P2, rep from * to last 7 sts, Tw3R, Tw3L, P1.
Row 29 K1, (P2, K2) twice, *P2, K3, P4, K3, P2, K2, rep from * to last 7 sts, P2, K2, P2, K1.
Row 30 P1, (K2, P2) twice, *K2, P3, C4F, P3, K2, P2, rep from * to last 7 sts, K2, P2, K2, P1.
Row 31 As row 29.
Row 32 P1, Tw3L, Tw3R, P2, *Tw3L, Tw4R, Tw4L, Tw3R, P2, rep from * to last 7 sts, Tw3L, Tw3R, P1.
These 32 rows form the patt.

project 9: oblong cushion

This beautifully textured, tailored cushion is an essential home accessory. It is knitted in a smooth Aran yarn and trimmed with a row of decorative buttons.

designer's tip

The stitch pattern gives a ruched effect. The knitting will smooth out and lay flat once it is blocked. Use the wet or spray blocking method and leave the knitting pinned out to size until it is completely dry.

Pattern

TO MAKE (made in one piece)
Using 5.5mm (size 9) needles cast on 98 sts.
Work in Cable Knot Check patt as follows:
Row 1 (RS) P4, K6, *P6, K6, rep from * to last 4 sts, P4.
Row 2 K4, P6, *K6, P6, rep from * to last 4 sts, K4.
Rows 3 and 4 As rows 1 and 2.
Row 5 P4, C6B, *P6, C6B, rep from * to last 4 sts, P4.
Row 6 As row 2.
Rows 7 and 8 As rows 1 and 2.
Row 9 K4, P6, *K6, P6, rep from * to last 4 sts, K4.
Row 10 P4, K6, *P6, K6, rep from * to last 4 sts, P4.
Rows 11 and 12 As rows 9 and 10.
Row 13 K4, P6, *C6B, P6, rep from * to last 4 sts, K4.
Row 14 As row 10.
Rows 15 and 16 As rows 9 and 10.
These 16 rows form the patt.
Rep them 11 times more, then work rows 1 to 8 again.
Now work ribbed band as follows:
Next row K2, *P2, K2, rep from * to end.
Next row P2, *K2, P2, rep from * to end.
Rep these 2 rows 3 times more, then work the first row again.
Cast off in rib.

YOU WILL NEED
• 350g Aran yarn in charcoal grey
• 5.5mm (size 9) knitting needles
• 5 buttons
• Oblong cushion pad

SIZE
36 x 57cm (14 x 22½in)

TENSION
1 patt rep of 12 sts to 7cm (2¾in) and 16 rows to 6.5cm (2½in), with patt opened out

TO FINISH

Block knitting to size (see designer's tip). Lay the knitting, with RS facing, on a flat surface and fold the top down, then fold the bottom up, overlapping the ribbing and the last half pattern (eight rows) – the pattern should match at the side seams. Pin the side edges. Join the side seams, working through all three layers at the overlap. Press seams lightly using a warm iron over a damp cloth. Turn the cover to the right side and insert the cushion pad. Slip stitch the first row of the ribbed band to the cushion cover, so leaving the band as a flap. Mark five button positions on the band, the first and last 3cm (1¼in) from the side seams and the others evenly spaced between. Working through both thicknesses, sew on the buttons to correspond with the markers.

project 10: knitting bag

Both practical and stylish, this knitting bag is worked using
two strands of tweed yarn together on large needles.

YOU WILL NEED
- 250g of Aran tweed yarn in green
- 6.5mm (size 10½) and 8mm (size 11) knitting needles
- Pair of long bag handles with a 28cm (11in) opening
- Fabric for lining
- Needle and matching sewing thread

SIZE
36cm (14in) wide by 35cm (13½in) long,
excluding handles

TENSION
1 patt rep of 13 sts to 9cm (3½in) and 17 rows to
10cm (4in) over cable patt on 8mm (size 11) needles
using two strands of yarn together

TO FINISH

Block back and front to size. Join side seams to within
10cm (4in) of hem. Press seams lightly using a warm
iron over a damp cloth. Turn the bag to the right side.
Thread the hem section of the front through and over
the opening in one bag handle. Sew the cast-off edge to
the first row of the hem section. Attach the other handle
to the back in the same way.

Pattern

BACK AND FRONT (alike)
Using 8mm (size 11) needles and two strands
of yarn together throughout, cast on 53 sts.
Work in Cable and Ridge patt as follows:
Row 1 (RS) P5, K4, *P9, K4, rep from * to
last 5 sts, P5.
Row 2 K1, P3, K1, P4, *K1, (P3, K1) twice,
P4, rep from * to last 5 sts, K1, P3, K1.
Row 3 P1, K3, P1, C4B, *P1, (K3, P1) twice,
C4B, rep from * to last 5 sts, P1, K3, P1.
Row 4 As row 2.
These 4 rows form the patt.
Cont in patt until work measures 33cm (13in)
from beg, ending row 4.
Change to 6.5mm (size 10½) needles.
Beg with a K row, work 8 rows st st for hem.
Cast off.

LINING

Cut a piece of lining fabric 34 x 72cm (13½ x 28in).
Fold fabric in half widthways and place a marker pin
on each side edge 11.5cm (4½in) down from the
short edges to mark the openings. Pin the side edges,
then taking a 1.5cm (½in) seam allowance, sew the
side seams up to the marker pins. Remove the marker
pins. Snip the seam allowance diagonally at the
bottom corners, then press open on both sides,
including the section above the stitching. Fold 1.5cm
(½in) to the wrong side along the two short edges
and press a fold. Insert the lining inside the bag with
the wrong sides together and the seams matching.
Pin in place. Slip stitch the lining to the bag along
the openings and across the top edges, gathering
the fabric slightly to fit.

project11: baby blanket

A soft, lightweight comfort blanket trimmed with fluffy pompoms – perfect for baby to cuddle up with.

YOU WILL NEED
- 300g super bulky yarn in cream for the blanket
- 50g DK yarn in mink for the pompoms
- 10mm (size 15) knitting needles
- Thin card
- Pair of compasses and pencil
- Scissors

SIZE
50 x 61cm (19½ x 24in) with cuff turned back

TENSION
1 patt rep of 10 sts to 11cm (4½in) and 12 rows to 8cm (3¼in) over cable patt

TO FINISH

Block knitting to size. Sew in the ends. Turn cuff to right side along fold line. Using 5cm (2in) diameter circles of card, make five pompoms (see page 133). Sew a pompom in the centre of each of the last reverse stocking sections worked along the cuff.

Pattern

TO MAKE (made in one piece)
Using 10mm (size 15) needles cast on 64 sts.
Work in Wavy Cable Check patt as follows:
Row 1 (RS) K1, P1, K4, P1, K1, *P6, K1, P1, K4, P1, K1, rep from * to end.
Row 2 P1, K1, P4, K1, P1, *K6, P1, K1, P4, K1, P1, rep from * to end.
Rows 3 and 4 As rows 1 and 2.
Row 5 K1, P1, C4F, P1, K1, *P6, K1, P1, C4F, P1, K1, rep from * to end.
Row 6 As row 2.
Row 7 K1, P6, K1, *P1, K4, P1, K1, P6, K1, rep from * to end.
Row 8 P1, K6, P1, *K1, P4, K1, P1, K6, P1, rep from * to end.
Rows 9 and 10 Rep rows 7 and 8.
Row 11 K1, P6, K1, *P1, C4F, P1, K1, P6, K1, rep from * to end.
Row 12 As row 8.
These 12 rows form the patt.
Rep them 6 times more, then work rows 1 to 6 again.
Next row K to mark fold line.
Beg row 7 to reverse knitting for cuff, patt 18 rows.
Cast off knitwise.

project12: handbag

An elegant, lined handbag for day or evening. Finished with neat, plastic handles and a fluffy trim – totally frivolous!

YOU WILL NEED
- 150g Aran yarn in charcoal
- 100g bulky yarn in black for lining
- 5mm (size 8) and 20mm (size 36) knitting needles
- Pair of 12.5 x 15cm (5 x 6in) U-shaped bag handles
- Fluffy trim, such as marabou or fake fur
- Needle and matching sewing thread

SIZE
29cm (11½in) wide by 23cm (9in) long, excluding handles

TENSION
1 patt rep of 12 sts to 5cm (2in) and 12 rows to 4.5cm (1¾in) over cable patt on 5mm (size 8) needles
8 sts and 13 rows to 10cm (4in) over Moss st patt on 20mm (size 36) needles

TO FINISH

Block back and front to size. Join side and cast-on edges. Press seams lightly using a warm iron over a damp cloth. Turn bag to right side. Fold the lining in half widthways and join the side seams. Position the handles centrally on the lining, just below the top edges. Sew the handles in place securely. Insert the lining inside the bag with the wrong sides together, the seams matching and the handles at the top. Pin the lining to the bag around the top edge, then slip stitch in position. Using a needle and sewing thread, sew a length of marabou or fake fur trim around the top edge.

Pattern

BACK AND FRONT (alike)
Using 5mm (size 8) needles cast on 68 sts.
Work in Cable Grid patt as follows:
Row 1 (RS) P2, *K4, P2, rep from * to end.
Row 2 K2, *P4, K2, rep from * to end.
Row 3 P2, *C4F, P2, rep from * to end.
Row 4 As row 2.
Row 5 P2, K4, *P8, K4, rep from * to last 2 sts, P2.
Row 6 K2, P4, *K8, P4, rep from * to last 2 sts, K2.
Row 7 P2, C4F, *P8, C4F, rep from * to last 2 sts, P2.
Row 8 As row 6.
Rows 9 to 11 As rows 5 to 7.
Row 12 As row 6.
These 12 rows form the patt.
Cont in patt until work measures 23cm (9in) from beg, ending row 4.
Cast off.

LINING (made in one piece)
Using 20mm (size 36) needles cast on 21 sts.
Cont in Moss st patt as follows:
Moss st row K1, *P1, K1, rep from * to end.
This row forms the patt.
Cont in patt until work measures 45cm (17½in) from beg. Cast off.

project13: floor cushion

Ideal as extra seating, this cosy, functional floor cushion is knitted in a super-bulky yarn on large knitting needles. A chunky tassel trims each corner.

designer's tip

Once you have inserted the cushion pad, the opening will need to be sewn with the right side facing. You can either slip stitch the opening taking small, neat stitches. Or, if you have been using mattress stitch to join the seams, where you are working on the right side, continue across the opening in the same way.

Pattern

FRONT
Using 10mm (size 15) needles and main colour, cast on 70 sts.
K 1 row and P 1 row.
Work in Staggered Cables patt as follows:
Row 1 (RS) K3, *P1, K6, rep from * to last 4 sts, P1, K3.
Row 2 P3, *K1, P6, rep from * to last 4 sts, K1, P3.
Row 3 K3, P1, K6, *P1, C6B, P1, K6, rep from * to last 4 sts, P1, K3.
Row 4 As row 2.
Rows 5 to 8 Work rows 1 and 2 twice.
Row 9 As row 3.
Row 10 As row 2.
Rows 11 and 12 As rows 1 and 2.
Row 13 K3, P1, C6B, *P1, K6, P1, C6B, rep from * to last 4 sts, P1, K3.
Row 14 As row 2.
Rows 15 to 18 Work rows 1 and 2 twice.
Row 19 As row 13.
Row 20 As row 2.
These 20 rows form the patt.
Cont in patt until work measures 50cm (20in) from beg, ending with a WS row.
K 1 row and P 1 row. Cast off.

BACK
Work as given for front, but start patt on row 11.

YOU WILL NEED

• 650g super bulky yarn in stone for the cushion
• 50g super bulky yarn in each of stone and charcoal grey for the tassels
• 10mm (size 15) knitting needles
• Square cushion pad
• Card for tassels

SIZE
60cm (23½in) square

TENSION
1 patt rep of 14 sts to 12cm (4¾in) and 20 rows to 15cm (6in) over cable patt, with patt slightly opened out

TO FINISH

Block back and front to size. Join seams leaving an opening on one edge to insert the cushion pad. Press seams lightly using a warm iron over a damp cloth. Insert the cushion pad and stitch the opening (see designer's tip).

Using stone and charcoal grey yarn, make four tassels (see page 132), wrapping one strand of each colour together around a 13cm (5in) length of card. Wrap a length of charcoal grey yarn twice around the tassel to secure. Sew a tassel securely to each corner of the cushion cover.

finishing techniques

Blocking and pressing, mattress stitch and backstitch – your handknits deserve a perfect finish.

Tassels, pompoms, twisted cord, fringing, buttons and thongs – enhance your knits with a touch of texture or surface embellishment.

lesson
13

blocking and pressing

Before you assemble a project it is essential to block and/or press all knitted pieces to size and shape. By using heat, water or steam you can even out any stitch irregularities and help curled edges lie flat, so giving your knitting a professional finish.

Always check your pattern instructions and the yarn label before pressing knitting – a beautiful piece of work can be ruined by using the wrong procedure.

steaming and pressing

Knitting worked in natural fibres, such as wool or cotton, and fairly plain textures can usually be steam pressed – always check your pattern and the yarn label. Pin the knitted pieces out to size on a blocking board using the grid on the fabric as a guide (see Tip, right), then place a clean, dry or damp cloth over the fabric and press lightly with an iron set at the recommended temperature – keep the iron moving and don't leave the full weight of the iron on the fabric. Never place an iron directly on a knitted fabric as you may burn the fibres and spoil the knitting.

Boldly textured fabrics such as cables should not be pressed as this will flatten the pattern. Instead, hold a steam iron over the cloth and allow the steam to pass through to the knitted fabric.

After pressing or steaming remove the cloth and leave the fabric to dry before removing the knitting from the blocking board.

Ribs can lose their elasticity when pressed, so unless they need to match the width of the fabric they are best avoided.

Once the pieces have been joined the seams will need to be pressed. Working on the wrong side, place a dry or damp cloth over the seams and use an iron set at the recommended temperature to lightly press the seams.

Do not press or steam synthetic yarns as the heat and steam will take the 'body' out of the yarn, making it limp – use the wet-spray method instead.

Tip

A blocking board is a very useful piece of equipment and is very easy to make. Place a sheet of wadding or curtain interfacing on a piece of board and cover with gingham fabric. Stretch the fabric, making sure you don't distort the checks, and secure it on the back with tape or staples. Lay the knitting on the blocking board and match the edges to the checks on the fabric to ensure they are straight.

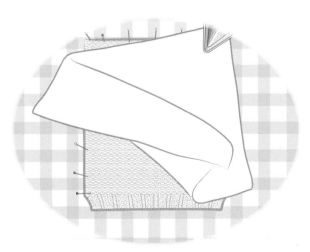

wet blocking

Use this method for yarn that cannot be pressed, textured or fluffy yarns and boldly textured stitch patterns. Wet the knitted sections gently by hand in lukewarm water. Carefully lift the knitting out of the water, gently squeezing out the water as you lift – do not lift it out while it is soaking wet as the weight of the water will stretch the knitting. To remove the excess water, lay the knitting on a towel and smooth out flat, then loosely roll up the towel from one end, applying a little pressure.

Unroll the towel and lay the knitting on a blocking board. Using long, rustproof glass-headed or knitting pins, pin the knitting out to size and shape, using the grid on the fabric as a guide. Leave to dry thoroughly to 'set' the fabric.

Cable fabrics are best wet blocked with the right side facing up. This enables you to mould the texture.

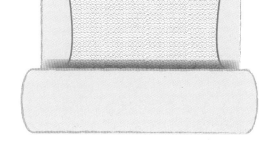

spray blocking

This method is similar to wet blocking and can also be used for yarns that cannot be pressed. Pin the sections of dry knitting out on a blocking board to size and shape, then use a water spray to thoroughly wet the knitting. Press gently with your hands to even out the fabric, then leave to dry before removing the pins.

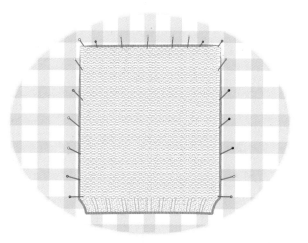

three-dimensional blocking

For projects worked in the round, use steaming, wet or spray blocking – choose the method most suited to the yarn and stitch pattern. Work on one side at a time, pinning the knitting out to size, taking care not to damage the stitches. Leave to dry, then repeat on the other side.

If you are blocking a small, circular item such as a hat or tea cosy, you can drape the piece over an upturned plastic pot or mixing bowl that is the right size. Wet the knitting and drape it over the form and leave to dry.

Tip

If you are not sure how to finish your knitting, use your tension swatch and the method you think suitable. If you are in any doubt, use the wet-spray method.

lesson 14 | perfect seams

One of the most important stages of a knitted project is the finishing – a beautifully knitted item can be ruined with poor seams. By following these simple techniques you can be assured of a professional finish every time. Refer to the finishing instructions on your pattern for the order of joining the pieces and, unless otherwise stated, use mattress stitch to join the seams.

mattress stitch

Mattress stitch produces an invisible seam and is worked on the right side of the knitting, making it easy to see how stitches and patterns are aligning.

Tip

If you have used a slubbed or boldly textured yarn for your project it may be difficult to join the seams with the same yarn. Try using a plain yarn in a similar weight and matching colour.

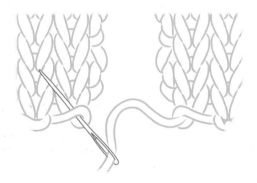

1 Place the two pieces to be joined side by side with the right sides facing and thread the end of yarn from the cast-on onto a tapestry needle. To start the seam, insert the needle from back to front through the corner stitch of the opposite piece.

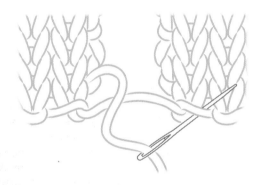

2 Make a figure-of-eight and insert the needle from back to front into the stitch the end of yarn comes from. Pull the yarn through and close the gap between the pieces of knitting.

3 Now insert the needle under the horizontal bar between the first and second stitches on the first piece, then under the horizontal bar between the first and second stitches on the second piece. Continue to work backwards and forwards between the pieces until a few rows have been worked.

4 Draw up the thread to form the seam – do not draw up too tightly or you will distort the fabric. Continue to join the seam in this way. When you reach the end, fasten off neatly by working a few stitches on the wrong side.

backstitch

Backstitch, one of the most commonly used stitches, can also
be used to join seams. This is worked with the right sides of the
knitting together and the wrong side facing you. To reduce bulk
on the seams and to ensure a neat finish, work the stitches near
the edge of the knitting.

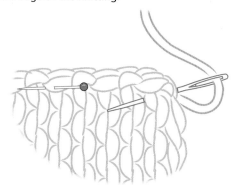

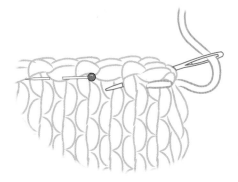

1 Pin the pieces to be joined with the right sides
together and the edges level. Thread a tapestry
needle with a length of yarn and work a couple of
small stitches on the right-hand edge of the back
piece of knitting to secure the yarn. Working one
stitch in from the edge insert the needle between
the first two rows of knitting from back to front.

2 Take the needle back over the first row and insert
it between the first row and the edge and pull
the yarn through. Now insert the needle between the
second and third rows and bring to the front, drawing
the yarn through.

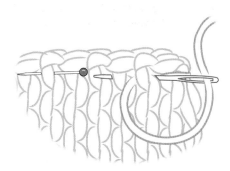

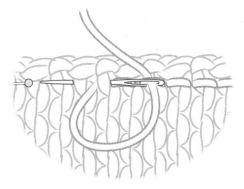

3 Take the needle back over the last row and insert
it at the point where the last stitch was worked,
then bring it to the front between the next two rows
and pull the yarn through.

4 Continue to work in this way, inserting the
needle at the point where the last stitch was
worked from front to back, then inserting it between
the next two rows from back to front. At the end
of the seam, work a couple of small stitches to secure
the yarn. Cut off the yarn.

lesson
15

tassels

Tassels are an ideal trimming for soft furnishings. Made in beautiful yarns such as wool, cotton, tape or ribbon they can add a touch of elegance or, in unusual materials such as raffia, leather and torn fabric, a touch of frivolity. Materials can be combined to great effect – to wool or cotton add a silky yarn for a subtle shimmer, or mix lengths of satin or organza ribbon with a ribbon yarn for sheer grandeur.

basic tassel technique

To make a simple tassel you will need yarn or cotton, card, a tapestry needle and sharp scissors.

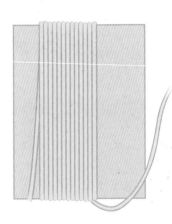

1 Cut a piece of card the required length of the tassel and about 8cm (3in) wide. Hold the card lengthways in one hand and hold the end of the yarn level with the bottom edge. Wrap the yarn evenly around the card to the thickness required, finishing at the bottom edge. Cut off the yarn.

2 Thread a length of yarn onto the tapestry needle and slip the needle under the loops along the top edge. Remove the needle and tie the ends, gathering the loops on the card loosely together. Do not trim the ends, as they can be used to attach the tassel.

3 Cut a long length of yarn. Carefully ease the loops off the card and hold them together. Knot one end of the length of yarn around the tassel about one third down from the top. Then wrap the yarn firmly around the tassel as many times as required to cover the knot.

4 Thread the end of the yarn onto the tapestry needle and take it up through the centre of the tassel. Use sharp scissors to cut through the loops at the bottom of the tassel and to trim the ends.

lesson 16 | pompoms

Pompoms are so simple to make and are perfect for trimming soft furnishings and garments – see Baby blanket on page 120. You can add single pompoms to the corners of cushions or dangle them in bunches at just one corner. A row of pompoms stitched along a cord makes a fun fringe for wraps or throws. You can make single-colour pompoms or add in extra yarn colours for multi-coloured variations.

basic pompom technique

To make a pompom you will need yarn, a pair of compasses, a pencil, card and sharp scissors.

1 On the card, use a pencil and a pair of compasses to draw a circle the size of the pompom. Now draw another circle inside it, about a third of the diameter of the first circle. Use the scissors to carefully cut around the pencil lines of the two circles, so forming a ring. Make a second ring in the same way.

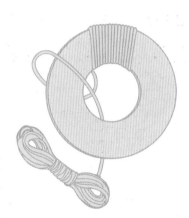

2 With the two rings together, wind yarn evenly around them – don't pull the yarn too tight. Continue to wind yarn until the centre hole is filled.

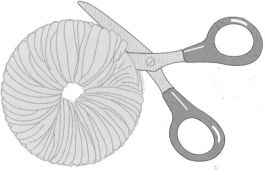

3 To form the pompom, insert a scissor blade between the card rings and cut the yarn around the outer edges. Slip a length of yarn between the rings and tie it tightly. Pull or tear off the card and fluff out the pompom. Trim any uneven ends, but leave the yarn tie for attaching the pompom to your work.

Tip

To make a decorative cord hanger for a pompom, make a small, thin twisted cord (see page 134) and use to tie around the strands of yarn in Step 3.

lesson 17

twisted cord

It's easy to make your own cords to use as ties, edgings and trims. You can use almost any kind of yarn – from fine mohair to chunky wool, or even leather thong or string. Either match your cord to your knitted fabric or go for a complete contrast. Alternatively, combine strands of yarn in different colours or textures.

making a twisted cord

Twisted cord requires long lengths of yarn – they should be three times the required finished length of the cord. Decide how thick you want your finished cord to be, then knot together enough lengths to make half that thickness.

To make a twisted cord you will need yarn, a tape measure, a wooden board, drawing pins (optional), a pencil and sharp scissors.

Tip

If you are using the cord as a tie (see Hot water bottle, page 82), tie a knot in both ends of the cord, then use sharp scissors to trim the ends. Untwist the yarn ends to form a small tassel.

1 Cut lengths of yarn three times the required length of the cord and knot them together at one end. Using a drawing pin, secure the knotted ends to a wooden board. Alternatively, tie the ends to a door handle or sturdy hook.

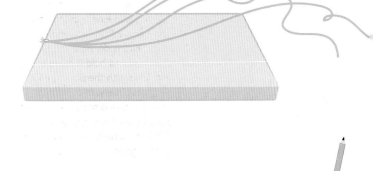

2 Tie the loose ends of the yarn around a pencil. Pull the yarn out straight and turn the pencil in one direction until the lengths of yarn are firmly twisted. Keep the threads fairly taut to ensure the twists are even.

3 Fold the twisted yarn lengths in half and allow the strands to twist around each other. Run your hand down the cord to even out the twists. Holding the ends securely, release them and knot together to secure. Trim the ends.

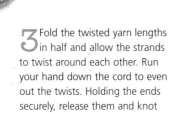
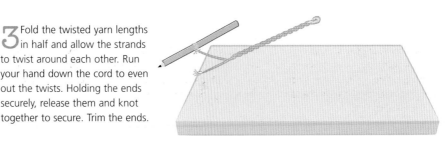

lesson 18

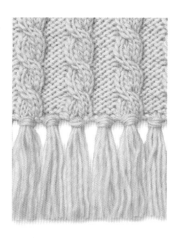

fringing

Fringing is a very versatile trim, adding a dramatic finish to plain edges – particularly on throws, wraps, scarves and cushion flaps. A fringe added to the bottom of a simple cable panel can be incorporated into the design to add a final flourish (see page 67). Work a fringe in one colour or texture, or add in extra colours or textures for added impact.

simple fringe technique

To make a simple fringe you will need yarn, card, sharp scissors and a crochet hook or hairpin.

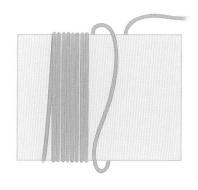

1 Cut a piece of card the required length of the finished tassel plus 2.5cm (1in) and about 15cm (6in) wide. Hold the card in one hand and hold the end of the yarn level with the bottom edge. Now wrap the yarn evenly around the card, taking the yarn over both sides for each single strand of fringing – a number of strands are used together to form each fringe.

2 Using a pair of scissors cut the loops along the bottom edge and lay the strands out flat. Repeat this process to make more fringing if required.

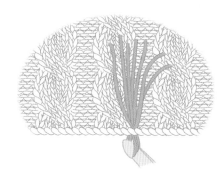

3 Take the number of strands desired and fold them in half, forming a loop. Insert a crochet hook or hairpin through the edge to be fringed from back to front, catch the loop and draw it through the knitting.

4 Use the crochet hook or hairpin to draw the ends of the strands through the loop. Pull the ends carefully to draw the knot up close to the edge. Repeat along the edge.

5 Place the fringe on a flat surface and lay the ends straight. Use sharp scissors to trim the ends evenly.

lesson 19 | adding buttons

Buttons can be used as simple fastenings or to add a decorative touch. There are so many beautiful buttons available that you will be spoilt for choice. If you are using buttons and buttonholes as a fastening make sure the button is the right size for the buttonhole – too small and it will keep coming undone; too big and you will stretch the buttonhole. Always start by marking the button positions as stated in the 'Finishing' section of the pattern.

buttons with two holes

A scattering of buttons will add extra interest to cable patterns. Plan out the position of the buttons before you start securing them in place. Buttons can be sewn or tied on following one of these simple techniques – choose the one best suited to your design.

Straight stitch

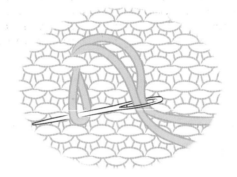

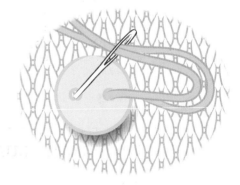

1 Cut a length of yarn or thread, fold it in half and thread the ends through a large-eyed needle. Working on the wrong side of the knitting, insert the needle through the knitting in the marked button position. Pull the ends of the yarn through, then insert the needle through the loop and draw up to secure.

2 Insert the needle from back to front through the knitting, then up through one hole of the button. Take the needle down through the other hole and through the knitting from front to back. Repeat as many times as required, then work a few small stitches on the wrong side to secure.

buttons with two holes

Beaded straight stitch

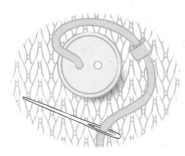

1 Thread a length of yarn or thread through a needle and work a few small stitches on the back of the knitting in the marked button position to secure. Insert the needle from back to front up through the knitting and up through one hole of the button. Now insert the needle through a bead.

2 Take the needle down through the other hole of the button from front to back. Repeat once more, then work a few small stitches to fasten off.

buttons with two holes

Tied

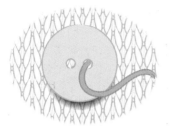  

1 Cut a length of yarn and thread one end through a large-eyed needle. Working on the right side, take the needle down through one hole of the button and through the knitting at the marked button position from front to back, leaving a 5cm (2in) end on the right side.

2 Insert the needle up through the knitting and the other hole of the button from back to front, then take the needle down through the first hole and back up through the second hole again.

3 Cut off the yarn leaving a 5cm (2in) end. Now tie a square knot, take the left end over the right and round, then take the right end over the left and around, and pull the ends to secure. Trim the ends as required.

buttons with four holes

Cross stitch

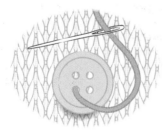 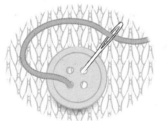 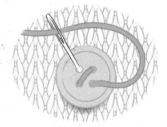

1 Cut a length of yarn and thread one end through a large-eyed needle. Working on the wrong side of the knitting, sew a few small stitches to secure the yarn at the button position. Now take the needle up through the knitting from back to front and through one hole of the button.

2 Lay the button in position on the knitting with the thread at the bottom left, and take the needle down through the hole at top right and through the knitting.

3 Bring the needle up through the knitting and through the hole at bottom right, then down through the hole at top left – this forms the first cross. Work another cross in this way, then fasten off by working a few small stitches on the wrong side of the knitting.

lesson 20

decorative thongs

Simple cables have contours that are perfect for highlighting with a decorative thong. There are many materials suitable to use as thongs – from lengths of ribbon to strings of glossy beads, and from braided lengths of yarn to strips of suede and leather. Whichever material you choose, make sure it is compatible with the yarn used.

Tip

If you are trimming an item that requires constant washing, make sure the thong you use is washable and the dye fixed. If you are in any doubt, remove the thong before washing.

adding a thong

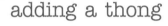

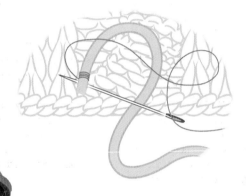

1 With the end of the thong level with the bottom of the cable, secure it in place on the wrong side of the knitting by working a few stitches over the thong with a sewing needle and thread.

2 Take the thong through the knitting to the right side at the bottom of the cable, then take it along the first curve of the cable and under the twist of the cable.

3 Continue to follow the curve of the cable, alternating one side and then the other, until you reach the top. Take the thong through to the wrong side and secure it at the top of the cable with a few stitches. Trim the end.

lesson 21 | aftercare essentials

It is important to take care of your finished knits – designs knitted in a quality yarn will last for many years if washed and cared for properly. Follow these simple guidelines to achieve the best results.

machine washing

Before you wash any item check the yarn label for washing instructions. For best results use soapflakes, mild detergent or specially formulated liquids. Many yarns are now machine-washable but do take care to select the correct cycle. To prevent the knitting shrinking or becoming matted or felted, wash on a delicate wool cycle with as little fast-spin action as possible.

hand washing

When washing your knits by hand, use warm water rather than hot and make sure the detergent is completely dissolved before submerging your knits. Handle them gently in the water – do not rub or scrub the knitting or wring it out, as this can felt the fabric.

Rinse well to get rid of any soap and squeeze out excess water – never lift a soaking wet item out of the water or you will stretch the knitting. Gently squeeze the water out as you carefully lift it out of the water. Lay the section out of the water on a surface while you handle the next section.

drying

It is important to remove as much water as possible before laying the knitting out to dry. Lay the item out flat on a towel and roll up from one end, applying a little pressure – the towel will absorb excess water.

Lay the damp item out flat on a dry towel and smooth it gently to size and pat to shape. Let it dry away from direct heat such as sunlight or a radiator and turn it occasionally.

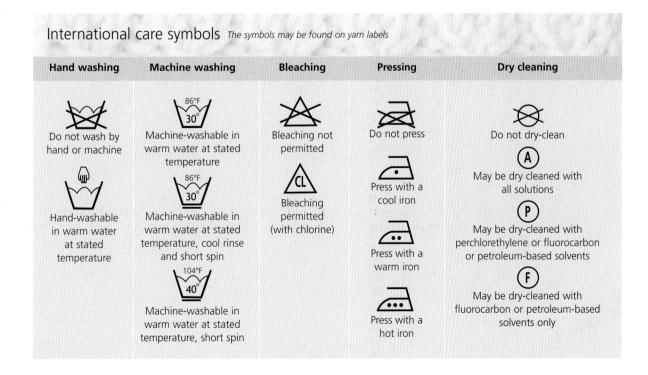

International care symbols *The symbols may be found on yarn labels*

Hand washing	Machine washing	Bleaching	Pressing	Dry cleaning
Do not wash by hand or machine	Machine-washable in warm water at stated temperature (86°F/30°)	Bleaching not permitted	Do not press	Do not dry-clean
Hand-washable in warm water at stated temperature	Machine-washable in warm water at stated temperature, cool rinse and short spin (86°F/30°)	Bleaching permitted (with chlorine) (CL)	Press with a cool iron	May be dry cleaned with all solutions (A)
	Machine-washable in warm water at stated temperature, short spin (104°F/40°)		Press with a warm iron	May be dry-cleaned with perchlorethylene or fluorocarbon or petroleum-based solvents (P)
			Press with a hot iron	May be dry-cleaned with fluorocarbon or petroleum-based solvents only (F)

abbreviations

K knit	**tog** together
P purl	**puk** pick up loop lying between needles and K into back of it
st(s) stitch(es)	**pup** pick up loop lying between needles and P into back of it
st st stocking stitch	**RS** right side
rev st st reverse stocking stitch	**WS** wrong side
patt pattern	**LH** left-hand
rep repeat	**RH** right-hand
beg beginning	**in** inch(es)
foll following	**mm** millimetre(s)
cont continue	**cm** centimetre(s)
tbl through back of loop	**yd(s)** yard(s)
yfd yarn forward	**m** metre
yon yarn over needle	
yrn yarn round needle	
sl slip	
psso pass slipped stitch over	
skpo sl 1, K1, pass slipped stitch over	

Chart symbols

□ K on RS rows, P on WS rows

● P on RS rows, K on WS rows

╱ K tbl on RS rows, P tbl on WS rows

○ yon or yrn to make a stitch on RS rows or on WS rows

— sl 1 with yarn at front

│ sl 1 purlwise with yarn at back

P wrapping yarn twice around needle

sl 1 purlwise with yarn at back, K2, psso the 2 knit sts

sl 2, drop next slipped st to front of work, then slip the same 2 sts back onto LH needle, pick up dropped st and K it

drop slipped st to front of work, K2, pick up dropped st and K it

B2 (Bind 2) yrn, P2, pass yrn over the 2 purl sts

B3 (Bind 3) sl 1 purlwise with yarn at back, K1, yfd, K1, psso the K1, yfd and K1

Br2 (Braid 2) sl 1 purlwise with yarn at back, K1, yarn to front and over needle, then psso the knit st and the yarn over needle

Cr3 (Cross 3) K into front of third st, then second st, then first st, slip 3 sts off LH needle together

Cr4 (Cross 4)

with yarn at back, sl 4 purlwise dropping extra loops, then with point of LH needle, pass the first 2 sts over the second 2; return the sts on RH needle to LH needle and K all 4 sts in the crossed order

Cr6 (Cross 6)

with yarn at back, sl 6 purlwise dropping extra loops, then with point of LH needle, pass the first 3 sts over the second 3; return the sts on RH needle to LH needle and K all 6 sts in the crossed order

W4 (Wrap 4)

K4, slip these 4 sts onto a cable needle and place at front of work; wrap yarn four times anticlockwise around these 4 sts, then slip sts back onto RH needle

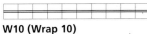

W10 (Wrap 10)

K2, (P2, K2) twice, slip these 10 sts onto a cable needle and place at front of work; wrap yarn three times anticlockwise around these 10 sts, then slip sts back onto RH needle

C4F (Cable 4 front)

slip next 2 sts onto cable needle and leave at front of work, K2, then K sts from cable needle

C4B (Cable 4 back)

slip next 2 sts onto cable needle and leave at back of work, K2, then K sts from cable needle

C6F (Cable 6 front)

slip next 3 sts onto cable needle and leave at front of work, K3, then K sts from cable needle

C6B (Cable 6 back)

slip next 3 sts onto cable needle and leave at back of work, K3, then K sts from cable needle

C8F (Cable 8 front)

slip next 4 sts onto cable needle and leave at front of work, K4, then K sts from cable needle

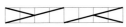

C8B (Cable 8 back)

slip next 4 sts onto cable needle and leave at back of work, K4, then K sts from cable needle

C7B rib (Cable 7 back in rib)

slip next 4 sts onto cable needle and leave at back of work, K1tbl, P1, K1tbl, then work (P1, K1 tbl) twice the sts from cable needle

C8B rib (Cable 8 back rib)

slip next 4 sts onto cable needle and leave at back of work, K1, P2, K1, then K1, P2, K1 from cable needle

C8F rib (Cable 8 front rib)

slip next 4 sts onto cable needle and leave at front of work, K1, P2, K1, then K1, P2, K1 from cable needle

Tw2R (Twist 2 right)

slip next st onto cable needle and leave at back of work, K1tbl, then P st from cable needle

Tw2L (Twist 2 left)

slip next st onto cable needle and leave at front of work, P1, then K tbl st from cable needle

Tw3R (Twist 3 right)

slip next st onto cable needle and leave at back of work, K2, then P st from cable needle

Tw3L (Twist 3 left)

slip next 2 sts onto cable needle and leave at front of work, P1, then K sts from cable needle

Tw4R (Twist 4 right)

slip next 2 sts onto cable needle and leave at back of work, K2, then P sts from cable needle

Tw4L (Twist 4 left)

slip next 2 sts onto cable needle and leave at front of work, P2, then K sts from cable needle

MB-1 (make bobble 1)

K into front, back, then front again of next st, turn and P3; turn and K3; turn and P3; turn and work sl1, K2 tog, psso – bobble completed

MB-2 (make bobble 2)

K1tbl, pick up loop lying between needles and K into back of it, K1tbl; turn and K3; turn and P3; turn and K3; turn and work s1, P2, psso the 2 purl sts – bobble completed

MB-3 (make bobble 3)

K1 and P1 into each of next 2 sts, turn and P4; turn and K4; turn and P4; turn and work skpo, K2tog – bobble completed

index

Credits

Yarn information

The following Sirdar, Rowan and Debbie Bliss yarns have been used for the knitting patterns in this book.

Mug and tea cosies (Project 1)
Sirdar Eco Wool DK 100% Undyed Virgin Wool 100m/109yd/50g

Placemat and napkin ring (Project 2)
Rowan Handknit Cotton 100% Cotton 85m/93yd/50g

Scarf (Project 3)
Debbie Bliss Alpaca Silk Aran 80% Alpaca/20% Silk 65m/71yd/50g

Storage basket (Project 4)
Sirdar Luxury Soft Cotton DK 100% Natural Cotton 95m/104yd/50g

Hot water bottle cover (Project 5)
Rowan Classic Baby Alpaca DK 100% Baby Alpaca 100m/109yd/50g

Hand muff (Project 6)
Rowan Pure Wool DK 100% Wool 125m/136yd/50g
Rowan Kidsilk Aura 75% Kid Mohair/25% Silk 75m/82yd/25g

Cushion and bolster (Project 7)
Rowan Cocoon 80% Merino Wool/20% Kid Mohair 115m/126yd/100g

Throw and cushion (Project 8)
Sirdar Eco Wool DK 100% Undyed Virgin Wool 100m/109yd/50g

Oblong cushion (Project 9)
Debbie Bliss Rialto Aran 100% Merino wool extrafine superwash 80m/87yd/50g

Knitting bag (Project 10)
Debbie Bliss Donegal Luxury Tweed 85% Wool/15% Angora 88m/96yds/50g

Baby blanket (Project 11)
Sirdar Big Softie Super Chunky 51% Wool/49% Acrylic 45m/49yd/50g. Sirdar Eco Wool DK 100% Undyed Virgin Wool 100m/109yd/50g

Handbag (Project 12)
Debbie Bliss Rialto Aran 100% Merino wool extrafine superwash 80m/87yd/50g balls. Rowan Biggy Print 100% Merino Wool 30m/33yd/100g

Floor cushion (Project 13)
Debbie Bliss Como 90% Merino wool/10% Cashmere 42m/46yd/50g

Go to the websites below to find a mail order stockist or store in your area.
www.sirdar.co.uk
www.knitrowan.com
www.debbieblissonline.com

Acknowledgements

I would like to thank the following people for their invaluable contribution in helping me to create this book.

Kate Kirby and Moira Clinch for giving me the chance to show my creative side. Katie Hallam for her excellent editing skills. Jackie Palmer for her creative design talent. Phil Wilkins for the clarity shown in his photography of the stitch patterns. Lizzie Orme for her beautiful photography. Kate Simunek for her lovely illustrations. Betty Willet for her thorough pattern checking. Special thanks to Sirdar, Rowan and Debbie Bliss for their generosity in supplying the gorgeous yarns for the projects.